From the Foreword by
PAUL TOURNIER

"Dr. Osborne's books—and this one in particular—
appear to me like the twin brothers of mine. There is
between us a family likeness, a common and constant
preoccupation—that of the human person, in order
to make the world more human. To be a person, isn't
it true, is to be neither an isolated individual, unconnected and irresponsible, nor a robot, an impersonal being drowned in the anonymous mass. To be a
person one must grow constantly. . . ."

*"Written in an interesting and readable style,
liberally leavened with anecdotes and case
histories . . . and with Dr. Osborne's own
brand of wry humor, it is a serious book with
a serious goal—*
the achievement of 'the whole person'.
—Peninsula Living

WITHDRAWN

you're in charge

Cecil G. Osborne

A KEY-WORD BOOK
Word Books, Publishers
Waco, Texas

124387

Scripture quotations marked RSV are from the Revised Standard Version of the Bible, copyright 1946 and 1952 by the Division of Christian Education of the National Council of the Churches of Christ in the United States of America, and are used by permission.

Scripture quotations marked NEB are from the *New English Bible*, © The Delegates of The Oxford University Press and The Syndics of The Cambridge University Press, 1961, 1970, and are used by permission.

Scripture quotations marked Phillips are from J. B. Phillips, The New Testament in Modern English, copyright © 1958 by J. B. Phillips.

The poem "Adam" by Nicholas Biel is reprinted from the Winter 59–60 issue by permission of *The Belou Poetry Journal*.

The quotations from *Life* magazine are © 1970 Time, Inc., and are reprinted by permission.

The quotations from *Guideposts* are © 1967 by Guideposts Associates, Inc., Carmel, New York, and are reprinted by permission.

The quotations from the San Francisco Chronicle are copyright Chronicle Publishing Company and are used by permission.

The situations and case histories described in this book are true, but the names have been changed to protect the individuals' privacy.

YOU'RE IN CHARGE

A KEY-WORD BOOK

Published by Pillar Books for Word Books, Publisher

First Key-Word edition published December 1976

ISBN: 0-87680-826-7

Library of Congress Catalog Card Number: 72-84168

Copyright © 1973 by Word Incorporated

Printed in the United States of America

Contents

Foreword

by Paul Tournier

IT IS with joy that I write this foreword in order to present this new book by Dr. Osborne. For several reasons:—

First, to express the deep affection which has linked me to him for a long time and to say how much I appreciate his person and his work.

And then, no doubt, many of those who read his book are also my own readers. So that it is an occasion for me to show them my gratitude, to say to them how much I was touched by the warm reception I was given by them in the United States.

And then, again, because we both belong to the Yokefellows Movement. He is actively devoted to it, while I participate only in spirit and admire from afar. In spite of this we are, it seems to me, like two oxen coupled together under the same yoke, who pull the same cart with the same step.

When I was a child we had a farm in the mountains in Haute-Savoie, and I knew how, despite its weight, to put the yoke on the neck of oxen in order to harness them to the harvest cart. Dr. Osborne will no doubt pardon me for this secular image which was suggested to me by the Yokefellows' name.

From my first meeting with him and the very personal manner in which he presented me to his church in Burlingame, I have felt strongly that we pulled the same cart together. That is, the cart of our common effort which is first to help men today whom our technical civilization too of-

7

ten tends to make sheep find a very personal blossoming, and then to seek in our faith the secret of the development of the person.

Also his books—and this one in particular—appear to me like twin brothers of mine. There is between us a family likeness, a common and constant preoccupation—that of the human person, in order to make the world more human. To be a person, isn't it true, is to be neither an isolated individual, unconnected and irresponsible, nor a robot, an impersonal being drowned in the anonymous mass. To be a person one must grow constantly. What does this mean?

Since my editors in New York and London have asked me to write a book on the problems of the retired and the aged, I can understand what it means better than ever. Because the retired people who are bored—sometimes almost to death—are the people whose narrow professional and social routine has gradually stripped them of all their creative personal imagination; they are people for whom the horizon and the heart have shrunk.

They may have had a good career, have been very overworked, have been able to handle capably the responsibilities entrusted to them. But on retirement they are no longer able to discover in themselves the resources to change over to the other more personal responsibilities. They do not know how to handle their freedom because the motivating force of their life was outside them, not internal, because they had developed their function, their professional role, but not their person.

All of a sudden these people have the tragic feeling that their life no longer makes sense. It is easy to see then that their preparation for retirement should have begun a long time before; that instead of shriveling up they should have grown spiritually all through their life, enriching their soul and spirit to give life a meaning which surpasses that of professional activity.

They are victims of our civilization which gives the preeminence to "doing" over "being," which does not value the man except in the function of his productivity. When one compares the soul of the child with its overflowing imagination with that of some retirees with their inner poverty, one realizes how much both education and modern professional life amputate the person instead of letting him blossom out. But what does it mean "to be," to develop one's being, his person?

These retired people, still capable but so withdrawn and passive, are victims of a present imbalance between the world of things and the world of persons. The world of things is tremendously developed, while that of persons loses its importance. For example, the physician today risks being absorbed in the very thing which is the illness—all the anatomical, physiological, and psychological phenomena which science explores, while he forgets that the patient is a person who has a very great need of making personal contact with him rather than being treated with technical remedies.

In order to help the patient grow as a person, the physician himself needs to be growing as a person. For no one is able to lead another further than he has been himself—as Dr. Plattner has said. And where does this growth come from? It was old Dr. Siebeck of Heidelberg who replied: "It is the vocation which creates the person." By vocation he meant not so much a trade or craft—the responsibilities which are conferred on us—but the inner call, the dialogue with God, which awakens in us the sense of our responsibility toward ourselves, our responsibility to grow. Growth, becoming adult, Freud defined as the passage from infancy to active life, as the fitness for social life, for marriage, and for work. But growth is also more than that; one understands it easily when he has made the transition from professional life to old age.

Yes! It is then that one perceives that there is an inner growth as important as social integration. The old person who no longer finds meaning in his life is the one who has lost both his cultural and intellectual growth and the growth of his heart, his achievement as a person. But he has already lost it, perhaps even in his youth. Professor Viktor Frankl of Vienna has made this grave illness of our time evident: the loss of meaning in life. He has called it the existential vacuum. He treats it by logotherapy which "has for a task," he writes, "the enlarging of the system of values of a patient, of making him see the fullness of possibilities of meanings and of values, of making him discover, so to speak, the total spectrum of values."

But, he adds immediately, with regard to this "question of values and meaning": "It comes back to the patient himself to respond to this double question: for what am I responsible? to what am I responsible? That is to say that an answer is only possible from a recovered personal responsibility." One can understand then why I connect the thought of Dr. Frankl with that of Dr. Osborne: it is by the grasp of the consciousness of our responsibilities that we discover the meaning of our lives, that we fill the existential vacuum which affects our present world.

As I do not know English well enough to understand Dr. Osborne's manuscript too well, I have had to resort to the collaboration of a young woman who carries heavy university responsibilities. I almost hesitated to ask for her help, for fear of burdening her further. However, her reaction struck me vividly. At the reading of this book, she told me, she realized that she felt more responsible for others than for herself and for her own personal development, that she gave herself so intensely to her work that she did not have more than one minute to herself, for personal growth, for reflection, for meditation.

Her situation seems to be more frequent than one would think. The professional responsibilities given to our charge eclipse our first responsibility, that of ourselves. Yes, my fellow-worker recognized this with great emotion: our first responsibility is to ourselves, to our inner realm, to our own person to enlarge and continually deepen it. This is the preliminary step which then prepares us to assume responsibility for others. One must develop himself in order to develop others!

The beautiful reaction of this young woman has taught me as much about the value of *You're in Charge* as if I were able to read it in detail. I do not doubt that it will help many other readers make fruitful discoveries in themselves. And that it will contribute to furthering this march toward personal accomplishment to which we are all summoned.

This then is why I am happy to present it to Dr. Osborne's readers.

PAUL TOURNIER
Geneva, Switzerland

Preface

FOR MORE years than I care to contemplate I was caught up in the murderous split between the sacred and the secular, the human and the divine. This dichotomy produced an undue amount of tension and conflict within me.

It helped a little to know that the Apostle Paul suffered from the same problem. He affirmed it in his letter to the Christians at Galatia, "The desires of the flesh are against the Spirit, and the desires of the Spirit are against the flesh; for these are opposed to each other. . . ."[1]

There is a bold New Testament statement I must have read a hundred times or more without its ever having registered. One day the passage stood out starkly from the page, and it was as though I had never seen it before. Jesus, speaking to the Pharisees, said, "Is it not written in your law, 'I said, you are gods'?"[2] I wondered why I had never dealt with it before. I could not recall ever hearing the statement used as the text for a sermon, nor even discussed for that matter. It was as though there was a conspiracy of silence—a tacit agreement to ignore it.

Perhaps we have been so concerned with affirming the divinity of Jesus that we are left with only our humanity. It is easier to excuse our faulty humanity than to accept the very threatening fact that we are gods. Most Christians are willing enough to refer to themselves or each other as children of God—a dependency relationship—but it is quite another thing to refer to oneself, or to another, as "a god."

11

I have become grossly irritated by hymns which affirm man's "vile condition." I refuse to sing the phrase in the hymn which tells us that Jesus died "for such a worm as I." There are days, or at least moments, when I do feel pretty "wormlike," but at a deeper level I am still aware of the awesome fact that spiritually I am made in God's image—that the deathless part of each human consists of the same divine essence as God.

I can still remember the relief I felt when I could accept at a fairly deep emotional level the knowledge that no failure of mine could ever be so great that God would love me less; and nothing "good" I might accomplish would cause Him to love me more. In other words, God loves that portion of himself in *me*, as in every human being. He has no other choice, for that is his nature.

Thus man is a god, whether he knows it or not. He was put in charge of this little planet, and more important, placed in charge of an inner kingdom over which he has exclusive control. He is the king of that inner kingdom. He has "made us kings and priests. . . ."[3]

So, man is in charge of his world, and in control of his own private inner kingdom. A part of the self wants to be dependent upon God who will "make everything right," and another part wants total, unconditional freedom. But when confronted with the frightening aspect of what this responsibility means, man recoils from it. Man wants the impossible—total freedom without responsibility. When things get rough most of us would like to abdicate, but this is not permitted in the plan God has established. Like it or not, *you're in charge!*

1.

You're in Charge

> "Human beings are not perfectible. They are improvable."
> —ERIC SEVAREID

IT TOOK Brenda seven years to complete four years of college. It wasn't that she lacked intelligence, but she had been told all of her life that she was stupid, and she had half believed it.

Her two alcoholic parents assured her over and over that it would be a miracle if she ever graduated from high school. When she expressed interest in going to college they laughed at her. Her high school teachers, with nothing to go on but her grades, also assumed that Brenda was not college material. They tried gently to discourage her.

What was it that kept Brenda at it for seven long years? When she graduated from college there was no great rejoicing. Father and mother were much too far gone in their alcoholism to be much impressed. I knew her first as a very lonely, insecure, frightened schoolteacher. She and her roommate had just broken up and gone their separate ways. She felt friendless and hopeless. At one point she was sure that suicide was the only way out.

I saw her in weekly counseling sessions for some months, then regularly in a sharing group. At first she would say to me, "I'm bad, aren't I?" At twenty-six she still felt "bad, worthless, inferior." This was the self-image she had derived from her tragic home enviroment.

I watched her growth with deep interest. Gradually she began to trust a few of us who knew her story and loved her. No one, she said, had ever loved her before. She tested our love pretty consistently at first.

Brenda had taken charge of her life and, frightened though she was, managed to make something of herself. When desperation and loneliness prompted her to seek professional counseling, I could sense her quiet determination to keep on growing. Within a matter of months the withdrawn, depressed young woman was reaching out to others and giving friendship and love. She is on the high road to fulfillment. She didn't wait for life to happen to her; she happened to life.

There are those who make an equally valiant start and then fall by the wayside. Barney was on his way out of town, trying to escape from two former wives who were demanding child support. On a whim he dropped into the lounge of our Yokefellow Center and picked up a book in the reading room. Something he read gripped him, and he sought me out. He told his story rather freely. He was a problem drinker and had been running all of his life. He had abandoned a wife in Europe while serving in the armed forces. He had another wife who wanted child support. There was much, much more that Barney felt a need to share.

Eventually in a Yokefellow group he shared some of the details of his unhappy life. No one offered any advice, but options were presented to him. Eventually he decided to stop running, to hold onto his present job, and start making restitution to the two women he had abandoned.

Week-by-week he seemed to like himself better as he cleaned up his life. He began to attend church, eventually joined, and was a faithful member for a year or two. Then he told me that he had found another church where they seemed to have a different and better "gospel emphasis." His enthusiasm in his new church home lasted a few months. Then, following his old pattern, he began to "run" again. His drinking pattern was resumed; eventually he appeared to be back about where he started. None of his new friends ever criticized or judged him, even when he dropped out of the group. He had been given unconditional love and acceptance. Barney, in charge of his own destiny, made choices that seemed totally self-defeating.

Psychologists are pretty well agreed that our basic emotional reactions to life are formed by the age of five or six. Some educational psychologists maintain that by the age of two and a half it is possible to predict how the child will be doing in school by the age of six.

At the same time, no one can define or set limits on free will. We simply do not know what a subtle combination of genes, circumstances, and will may produce. Within the general framework of heredity, environment, and circumstances, we *do* have some crucial choices to make. We are in charge. We are responsible—not for genetic flaws or bad environment—but for the use we make of whatever mental and emotional endowment we possess.

Judy told me matter-of-factly of the wretched home in which she was reared. Anything seemed better than the bleak, unloving atmosphere in which she lived, so one day when she was fourteen she put a few of her things in a shopping bag and walked away from home. She spent that night sleeping in an alley. The next morning, leaving her few possessions in an alley doorway, she went down the street to get a cup of coffee. When she returned, her shopping bag was gone. Now she had neither home, money, clothes nor friends. She walked around aimlessly for a few hours. A man paused to ask her if she needed help. She told him of her plight, and he took her home where he and his wife provided the warm, accepting environment she had never known. The man found a job for her, and from that time on she was on her own.

Judy had a very weak self-image. No one had ever loved her or given her a sense of self-worth. When she had a number of rather unusual opportunities, she couldn't accept them because she just didn't feel worthy.

Eventually she married a man who was her inferior in every way. There was no love because Judy had never learned how to give or receive love.

In her thirties, stirred by some inner burning desire to have a better life, she told me her story. In a Yokefellow sharing group, no one could detect the slightest trace of self-pity, just a quiet determination to find out who she was and how she could be more, love more, and be more deeply fulfilled. At this point she is working toward that goal. She assumed total responsibility for her own life from the day when, at fourteen, she walked out into the world.

Some elusive quality in her personality suggests that she will achieve her goal.

What part does chance play in our lives? Not every lonely, wandering girl can be guaranteed the appearance of an earnest Christian man at the crucial moment. Where does our genetic wiring fit in, our programming by parents and others during the formative years?

It had been decided by the teachers, in consultation with the principal, that Rod was mentally retarded. The parents had been informed that very shortly he would be placed in another school where he would "fit in better" with other mentally retarded children.

The day before the transfer one of his teachers took a few minutes to talk to Rod. The frightened boy opened up to this warm, friendly man. The teacher then announced to the principal that Rod was not mentally retarded, just frightened out of his wits. An abusive father had made him fearful of all authority figures, rendering him mute in their presence.

Rod was in his early forties when I first met him. He was a Ph.D. and an ordained minister, doing a magnificent job in a church-related field. One teacher's interest and concern altered the entire course of his life.

It would be wrong to assume that we are totally responsible for everything that happens to us. The Apostle Paul bore no responsibility for the tragic events that befell him. He was shipwrecked, imprisoned, beaten, and left for dead, deserted by friends, and hounded by his enemies. At no point do we hear him asking, "What have I done to deserve this?"

But Paul did accept responsibility for being in charge of his own life. He did not claim any personal credit for being able to endure innumerable hardships. He said that with Christ's strength added to his own he could face anything.

What part does God play in our destiny? Where is God when disaster strikes? It is interesting that when blessed by good fortune, no one is heard to ask, "Where was God when I was so richly blessed?" Rather we assume that we deserve the good.

How Can One Know God?

Perhaps the basic question is not so much what part God plays in our destinies, but, how can we know him? Fortunately we are not commanded to understand God, but to love him; and knowing that God is like Christ, it is easier to approach him. How tenderly Jesus touched, healed, forgave those who came to him. He came, "not to condemn the world, but that the world might be saved through him."[1] Many of us have a hard time believing that God is really like this.

My early childhood was spent in a religious atmosphere that was judgmental, pharisaical, and moralistic. I can still recall how, at the age of four or five, I learned that God could see through brick walls. That frightened me half out of my wits, for I was a very wicked little boy—or so I felt. If God saw all that was going on even behind closed doors, I was doomed. If God was at all like my father, I would be loved if I were good, but I would catch it if I were bad. And only God and I knew the full extent of my childish depravity.

How many thousands of judgmental, condemnatory sermons I sat through! The standards were set higher and higher, but no one ever told me specifically how to attain those standards. The peril of falling into the hands of an angry God was very great. My guilt complexes had guilt complexes. An unending stream of evangelists came to town, and as I look back on it, it seems to me that every one of them talked about "secret sins." The accusing finger inevitably came to rest on me: "Be sure your sins will find you out."[2] I wondered if that meant that I was supposed to leap up and blurt out my list of terrible sins, or that in due time I would be exposed. And when would that be?

We were supposed to "measure up," to be "just like Jesus," and God knows I wasn't just like Jesus. I was certain I could never be because I had a black heart. I knew it was black because they told me so, and some of the songs we sang reiterated it. But if we could just let Jesus come in, he would make that black heart clean. I tried but he never came, or if he did I didn't know it. In time, around the age of twelve, I "went forward" at a revival meeting and was baptized. I was now a professing Christian and things would be different. I wouldn't have the same temptations, or it would be easy to overcome them. He would give me strength to face all evil. But the day after I was baptized I realized I was no different, except that I now had to live up to a still higher standard and "live like a Christian," which to me meant sinless perfection. I didn't make it.

No one ever told me what to do about guilt, except to confess it and be cleansed. I confessed my sins and felt just as guilty as before. No one explained that nearly all of the guilt that bothered me was false guilt.

One does not overcome that sort of background all at once. At least I didn't. I expect I shall not, in this life, recover completely from the damage done by my early childhood conditioning. Discovering later that God was like Jesus did not completely liberate me. Intellectually I had it all straightened out, but emotionally I still had the scars, as do millions of others who experienced a judgmental home and church environment.

The way Jesus dealt with a greedy tax collector, a prostitute, the sick, the weak and faltering, tells me something of the nature of god, for God is like Jesus. Catching a glimpse of the love and compassion of God, as revealed in Jesus, I can sense that there is vastly more of God than I shall ever be able to perceive fully, but I love what little of God I can grasp.

An ancient mystic has said, "The whole earth is the garment of the Lord; release it and receive it back as a gift." I pondered that for days until its full meaning burst upon me. You cannot touch a leaf, or walk a mountain trail, or wade in the ocean without touching the garment of the Lord—his glorious Planet Earth. And when you touch, lovingly and with awe and wonder, the face of a child, you are touching God, or at least a manifestation of him. To love the manifestations of God—his earth and its wonders—is to love him. To love his other children is to love him. To forgive them, and be forgiven by them, is to enter into the joy of the Lord. To love his laws and precepts is to love him.

For some obscure reason not now clear to me, I used to spend a considerable amount of time trying to convince others that "God is a person." Rather than trying to make the infinite God personal and thus limit him, let it be said that God is Spirit (beyond our human comprehension to understand fully), but he *becomes personal through persons, supremely so in Christ*. Jesus was the supreme manifestation of God. To a lesser degree we see God manifested in other persons. Each of us is in some degree a manifestation of God, just as is every created thing.

To fail to love another human being is a failure to love a manifestation of God. To feed the hungry, clothe the naked, visit the sick is the same as ministering to Christ, since each of these needy humans is a manifestation of the divine.

Can God Be Defined?

Any term used to describe God is faulty, in that it limits him. Cosmic Mind, Divine Mind, Creator, Father, Ground of our Being—these or any others have semantic connotations which imply different things to different people. Besides, no human term can fully describe or define the infinite. So, baffled, we turn to Jesus the Christ. Now we can get our hands on something or Someone understandable in human terms. God is like Jesus. That we can begin to understand. "Ground of our Being" is meaningless to me. "Father" reminds me, at a feeling level, of a human father who was often irritable and sometimes rejecting. "Divine Mind" strikes me as somewhat impersonal. "Creator" connotes a building contractor a bit too busy with his cosmos to be concerned about a sparrow's broken wing. But Jesus is different! I see him as both strong and tender. I envision him laughing with the Twelve, else how could he have expressed the hope "that my joy may be in you, and your joy complete"?[3] I sense that he smiled gently, lovingly into the frightened eyes of that woman flung at his feet by the judgmental Pharisees; and in his smile I know—I know!—there was forgiveness and acceptance. She would never forget that look!

This we can get hold of—this Jesus of strength and tenderness, assurance and love. And along with Thomas we can fall at his feet and declare, "My Lord and my God."

I was driving along a freeway one day feeling at peace with the world. Suddenly there flashed into my mind the words, "Open thou mine eyes, that I may behold wondrous truths out of thy law."[4] Then there floated up from some inner depths the words, "Great peace have they who love

19

thy law and nothing shall disturb them."[5] I looked up these two statements the next day. Both are loose quotations from the 119th Psalm, but separated by many other verses. They really belong together, for they are related, profound cosmic truths. To be open to the truths of God, to welcome them, to seek and love these divine universal principles, is of supreme importance.

And the truths of God are revealed not so much in legalistic dos and don'ts, but in the person of Christ. Christianity is not a religion of creeds and doctrines, but a Way of life, lived in fellowship with Christ.

I have a Jewish friend who, so far as I know, had never attended a Christian church, or even read the New Testament. He was in a half-waking state one day, when suddenly the overwhelming conviction came to him: "Of course Jesus is the Messiah! How could I have ever believed otherwise!" He has never doubted this. It was not reason or logic or human persuasion which brought him to this revelation, but an upward surge of inner truth which is in all of us. "God is a work in you, both to will and to work for his good pleasure."[6]

Who's in Charge Here?

"God is at work." But from another point of view, God has already done everything he intends doing. He has put into operation every principle and made available the power to answer every human need. It is not necessary for him to think it over, or test you, or delay, or push any buttons to answer your prayers. He has taken the initiative. Now it's all up to you. *You're in charge!*

Adam was placed in charge of the garden. Take this literally or symbolically; it doesn't really matter. The truth is what matters, which is that God has put us in charge of our world. *You're in charge!* You are in charge of your destiny. You are responsible—within certain limits—for what happends to you. The limits, of course, are genetic and environmental. All of us have our limitations, and God understands all about that and makes allowances. But you are in charge of your decisions, your choices, your ultimate fate. The initiative is yours.

You can bring your will and actions into harmony with the cosmic laws established before the foundations of the

20

earth were laid, or you can reject these beneficent laws and principles. The choice is yours.

In a ministers' Yokefellow group we were dealing with our own personal feelings about God, each other, and ourselves. Someone spoke of "the will of God," and we discussed it at some length. Finally I said, "This is all very intellectual and theological. We think nice, scriptural, appropriate things about God's will. The important thing is: do I want the whole will of God in my life? If not, do I want his will part of the time, 'sort of,' or do I fear the will of God?" Then I added, "One might even say, 'I *want* to want the will of God.' Let's find out where we are, at a feeling level, on this matter."

Each man present, with one exception, told what he felt about the will of God in his life. No one could say with absolute certainty that he always wanted the whole will of God. For, as one man said, "If, I did, why would I act the way I do sometimes?"

When they had, in honesty and humility, told where they were in relation to the will of God, the group members turned to the one who had not spoken. He began to talk, and for ten minutes he preached a sermon, quoting many scripture passages. It was an obvious evasion, but he was so engrossed in his sermonette that he didn't observe our amusement. Eventually I said, "Hold it, Ted. You're preaching, and that's a 'no-no, in this group. We want feelings."

He started again, this time wringing his hands. He quoted more Scripture. Someone stopped him, gently but firmly: "You don't have to share anything with us, but if you do, let it be an honest feeling, not last Sunday's sermon." Finally, after fifteen or twenty minutes of anguished evasion he said, "Well, I do—I really *do want* the will of God, the whole will of God. But I want to stay in Northern California!" The group laughed, not so much at him, as at our own humanity—for each of us had already admitted that in some degree we wanted to hold out a little portion of our own wills.

The evasive minister was speaking for most of humanity. There's no question but that we want God's blessings, but wanting his will is another matter. This business of surrendering totally to God's will can be terribly frightening. It is as if one would be robbed of his own identity, without choices, and become a kind of saintly, compliant robot no longer permitted to make decisions.

The shattering truth is quite the opposite. God will *not* rob us of our autonomy. He will not take charge and tell us what to do. He will not override our wills. He insists that we accept responsibility for our own decisions. *We* are in charge.

Adam was free to obey or disobey God. He had unlimited freedom to operate as he chose, so long as he obeyed the general outline of the command of God: "have dominion over [it]," but "you shall not eat of the fruit of the tree which is in the midst of the garden. . . .'"

Just as Adam was free, so we are free—and in charge of our own destiny. Instead of a blueprint ("God's will for my life") there is open, unlimited freedom to choose our own course of action. One may "tune in" and receive a gentle sense of "oughtness," a feeling of being guided or led, but at any point in life man is free to choose.

ADAM
by Nicholas Biel

On the third day I was dust,
ordinary common dust
like you see on a country road
in a dry spell nothing
expected of me, me
expecting nothing either.

On the sixth day he comes
along and blows. "In my own
image too," he says like he
was doing me a favor.

Sometimes I think if he'd
waited a million years
by then I'd been tired
maybe being dust
but after only two, three
days, what can you expect? I
wasn't used to being
even dust and he goes
and makes me into Man.

He could see right away
from the expression on my face

I didn't like it so
he's going to butter me up
he puts me in this garden only
I don't butter.

He brings me all the animals I
should give them names—what
do I know of names? "Call
it something," he says,
"anything you want," so I
make names up—lion, tiger,
elephant, giraffe—crazy,
but that's what he wants.

I'm naming animals since
5 A.M. In the evening I'm tired
I go to bed early, in the
morning I wake up, there she
is sitting by a pool
of water admiring herself.

"Hello, Adam," she says, "I'm
your mate. I'm Eve." "Pleased

22

to meet you," I tell her
and we shake hands.
Actually I'm not so pleased—
from time immemorial
nothing, now rush rush rush;
two days ago I'm dust,
yesterday all day I'm naming
animals today I got a mate
already.

Also I didn't like the way
she looked at me
or at herself in the water.

Well, you know what
happened, I don't have to tell
you, there were all those fruit
trees—she took a bite, I
took a bite, the
snake took a bite and
quick like a flash—
out of the garden.

Now I'm not complaining;
after all, it's his garden,
he don't want nobody eating
his apples, that's his business.

What irritates me is
the nerve of the guy.

I didn't ask him to make me
even dust; he could have left
me nothing like I was before—
and such a fuss for one lousy
little apple not even ripe
(there wasn't that much time
from Creation, it was
still Spring). I didn't
ask for a mate, I didn't
ask for Cain, for Abel, I

didn't ask for nothing but
anything goes wrong, who's to
    blame?
. . . Sodom, Gomorrah,
    Babel, Ararat . . .
me or my kids catch it,
. . . fire, flood, pillar of salt.
"Be patient," Eve said, "a
little understanding. Look
he made it, it was his idea,
it breaks down, so he'll fix it."

But I told him one day.
"You're in too much of a
hurry. In six days you make
everything there is, you expect
it to run smoothly?
Something's always going to
happen. If you'd a
    thought
first, conceived a plan,
consulted a specialist, you
wouldn't have so much trouble
all the time."

But you can't tell him
nothing. He knows it all.

Like I say, he means well
but he's a meddler and
he's careless. He could
have made that woman so
she wouldn't bite no apple.

All right, all right,
so what's done is done
but all the same he
should have known better
or at least he could have blown
on other dust.

The author of this poem is expressing a feeling which
many humans experience on occasion. It is a reluctance,
conscious or unconscious, to accept responsibility for life.

Job in his despair cursed the day he was born. Later he rises to the heights with the declaration, "Though he slay me, yet will I trust him."[8] Such ambivalence is a part of our humanity.

It has been years since I saw the film *Ben Hur*, but the final scene still stands out vividly in my memory. In the half-light of a storm-darkened sky you could see in the distance three crosses silhouetted on a hill. Moving closer, the focus was upon the cross in the center. The man's face was never visible, but as the landscape was illuminated by repeated flashes of lightning, you saw that lonely figure move in silent agony.

It was raining and dark except for lightning flashes. The crowd had all but disappeared. In those intermittent bursts of light you could see a pool of rainwater forming at the base of the cross. Suddenly a drop of blood fell into it, and was diffused. Then another, and another, and still another drop until, as you watched, the pool became tinged with red.

The rain continued to fall, and the pool enlarged, finally turning crimson as the flow of blood increased. Then the enlarging pool began to overflow into a smaller pool just below it. The storm continued, and the second pool enlarged. It began to overflow into another forming just below it. Your eye followed that bloodstained water flow on down to a third pool, until that overflowed into a tiny stream. It in turn flowed on until it met a larger stream.

Imagination followed that stream to the place where it met a river, and on to where the river poured into the sea. Eventually that glood-tinged water would touch the shore of every continent and island on this planet—symbolic of the spread of the good news, the love of God.

It is not the literal blood of Jesus which "cleanses us from all unrighteousness," but what the blood represents— the limitless, redeeming, unbelievable love of God revealed in Jesus Christ, the Son of God. I do not try so much to understand that love, as to accept, and then to become a channel through which it can flow into other lives.

Yes, there is Someone "out there." But he dwells "in here" too; for we are made in his image. He has placed within us a portion of the divine essence—pure spirit. And having made us in his own image, he has made each of us responsible. *You're in charge.*

2.

Who Am I?

> "I went to Europe to find myself, but I wasn't there."
>
> —ANONYMOUS

AT DOZENS of retreats, and elsewhere, I have asked the question, "Who are you?" The response is usually one of puzzlement, as though it is an absurd or irrelevant question.

A woman responds, "I am a wife and mother."

"No," I reply, "you have simply described your role. That is not your identity."

A man says, "I have spent thirty-eight years as a wholesale grocer. I live and breathe the grocery business. So far as I'm concerned, that—and being a good father, church member and decent citizen—is identity enough." He has named his vocation, not his identity.

Someone else responds with, "I am mind and body."

"You left out the soul," adds another.

"All right, so I'm a mind, body, and immortal spirit, and I have a role as worker, parent, and citizen. How's that?" asks someone else.

But a mood of bewilderment usually falls on the group as they begin the search for their true identity. Who am I?

It is easier to define what one is not. "I" am not a physical body, for that is temporal and will one day cease to exist. "I" am not parent, child, employee or, employer—for these are roles and relationships.

At a ministers' retreat led by a friend of mine, the men got to know each other intimately during the week, and a spirit of love and good will pervaded the sessions. It was a relatively small group, and in the sharing sessions they had developed a deep bond of fellowship. Their love and openness were beautiful by Saturday night. But Sunday morning the mood had mysteriously changed. The men were quiet, subdued, tense. Occasional barbed witticisms flashed back and forth, thinly veiled bits of hostility.

Finally someone said, "What is going on here? Last night we all loved one another. This morning all of our good will and love have disappeared. What happened?" In the ensuing discussion they found the answer. It was Sunday morning, and they were not in their pulpits! They had no real identity, other than their ministerial role.

This is a very common occurrence. It is seen perhaps most often with mothers whose children have left home, and in men who retire. In the case of a mother, it can be an understandable but painful predicament. For twenty or more years she has been "mother." That was her chief role, and unconsciously she assumed this as her identity. Now with no children to mother, if she has developed no concept of her true identity, she is nothing. She still has a husband, but the mother role for her may have been the chief one, her main source of achieving satisfaction. And "being a wife" describes a relationship or role, not an identity.

I watched with deep concern as a long-time friend of mine approached retirement. He had spent forty years with a large national corporation and risen to a position of great responsibility. The week before his retirement he was in charge of a far-flung enterprise. The following week he was a bewildered ex-vicepresident of a large concern, walking around his beautiful yard watching the gardener. A few months later at a social function I saw this formerly gay, dynamic man slumped in a chair wearing a dazed expression. He lived for a few years, but never found any thing worthwhile to do. I watched him die slowly, inexorably.

Like millions of others, my friend had confused his role as industrialist with his identity. If he had been asked who he was, he would have replied, "I am vice-president of my firm." The fact that it was one of the largest in the world and his consequent sense of achievement were not enough to give him a sense of identity. He remained only an "industrialist," a "vice-president." These are titles, not an identity.

You are Gods

In one group where this question of "Who are you?" was posed, eventually someone gave a technically correct answer: "I am a child of God." Everyone agreed.

"That's fine," I said, "but why is it we are so willing to call ourselves children of God, but not 'gods'?"

The group looked shocked.

I then quoted the statement of Jesus, as recorded in John 10:34, " 'you are gods.' " Jesus was responding to the Pharisees who were on the verge of stoning him because he had said, "I and the Father are one." When they accused him of blasphemy, he asked, "Is it not written in your law, . . . 'you are gods'?" He was quoting from the 82nd psalm.

Most of us are willing to accept the idea that we are "Children of God," for this puts us in a dependency role. Children are not expected to assume full responsibility. There is always a mother and father who are the ultimate authorities, and who will be "in charge."

Most Christians refuse to refer to themselves as "gods," for this implies, at first, a kind of blasphemy, and then a bewildering sense of responsibility! Who wants to accept the responsibility of acting like a god!

Who am I? I am a center of *pure consciousness*. I am a portion of the divine essence. I am, at the core of my being, made of the same spirit-essence of which God is composed, as a child consists physically of the same blood and tissue as his parents. I am a being who is "aware of being," a self who is aware of being a self, as no animal can be. I am infinite spirit encased in a finite body which will return to dust. Whether we call this inner god self, spirit, soul, or a portion of the divine essence, we are simply groping for finite words with which to express the infinite.

The difficulty we have with this concept of being gods is the ageless conflict of the human and divine. The Apostle Paul, speaking of his own experience, said that the spirit is in conflict with the body, and the body with the spirit.[1] If the meaning of life is growth and fulfillment of our destiny, then the *ultimate* meaning of life is *to accept and bring into*

harmony both our humanity and our divinity. I have difficulty in accepting my humanity fully and I cannot accept
my divinity completely. There are many aspects of my humanity which I reject or dislike. Thus I am not "fully human." All self-rejection is based in part upon rejection of
one's humanity, but it is even more difficult to accept at a
feeling level the astounding statement of Jesus that "you
are gods."

Evidence of our unconscious rejection of this is found in
the fact that almost no one can recall ever having heard a
sermon on this teaching of Jesus. It is far too threatening a
concept to deal with. It is much easier to settle for the
minutia of morality, or social action, or ethical conduct. In
fact, it is far less threatening to many persons to join a
protest march than to sit down for an hour and deal with
the shattering revelation that "I am a god."

Jesus' Humanity and Divinity

No one has ever or will ever fully understand or explain
the Incarnation, the idea that Jesus was fully man and fully
God. But it is apparent from his life and teaching that he
accepted completely both his humanity and his divinity. He
was tempted at every point where any human can be
tempted. He felt every urge and surge of emotion which
any normal human being can experience, both physical and
mental, emotional and spiritual. He demonstrated what a
person could be who was truly human, and he merged this
with a full acceptance of his divinity. In the full acceptance
and merging of humanity and divinity he could be the Messiah, the Promised One, the Redeemer, the "Way-Shower."

Over a hundred different names or titles are given him in
the Old and New Testaments in an effort to express this
Perfect One, and all fall short, as human words must always fail to express perfection.

Let's have a look at our humanity. We are physical
beings, akin to the animals. Like them we have five senses—sight, touch, hearing, taste, smell. Partly because of
the gross immorality of the pagan world, some Christian
groups began to equate sensuality with sexuality, and sexuality with immorality. Our Puritan ancestors fell into this
trap.

But let's reexamine the God-given senses. They are channels through which God can speak to his own spirit which he has put within us. To watch a magnificent sunset, to walk on the beach or stroll along a mountain path, to touch a beautiful child, to be thrilled, stirred, inspired, and made to feel serene, reverent, awestruck by sight and sound and touch, is to let the physical work in harmony with the spiritual.

For me, to sit or lie in a field of wild flowers overlooking the ocean, smelling the salt spray and the flowers, becoming one with the boundless ocean, watching the clouds drift across a blue sky—all this can be an act of worship, a blending into the "isness" and oneness of God. Then, if over a portable radio I can hear a favorite symphony, and later, when hungry, can eat—this is a sensual, spiritual, human, divine experience. Why deny the sense or sensuality? Why insist on the murderous split between the human and the divine, if the goal is to accept fully our humanity and our divinity?

Part of our difficulty in accepting our humanity is that the two strongest God-given drives are aggression and sex. They are such powerful instinctual drives that they cause all manner of trouble if uncontrolled. Hence, from the dawn of time rigid tribal codes have been established to control these emotions.

Children learn early in life that there are many "no-no's." Anger is wrong and sexual curiosity is bad, according to many misguided parents. The lot of the parent is not an easy one, for uncontrolled anger is dangerous and sexual promiscuity is disastrous. So, one way or another, our two strongest drives are either repressed or labeled "bad." In denying or labeling "bad" these two powerful, God-given drives, we deny a large portion of the self.

All of our sensations are valid and God-given: pain, awareness, grief, joy, happiness, hunger, anger, love, jealousy, and all the rest. It is not the emotion that is evil or destructive, but the improper use of it. This brings us inevitably to the matter of responsibility. Why does God permit sin, suffering and sorrow? If he is running the world why does he allow war? Or hunger and starvation? If he is a God of love, why doesn't he do something about such evils?

Thus the child in us asks a Celestial Daddy to take over, to make things right, to make all the bad people good, and all the good people nice, because that would make life easier for us. Why did God allow the Dark Ages to hang over Europe like a black pall, with plague, ignorance, and crime running rampant? Why, for that matter, does he allow anyone to do anything evil or destructive?

The answer is simple and terrifying. "You are gods." *We are in charge!* It is our world. The pagan philosopher Marcus Aurelius wrote of "the deity which is planted in thee" in A.D. 170. Yet roughly twenty-five hundred years after the psalmist declared, "You are gods," and nearly two thousand years after Jesus reaffirmed it, Christians are still reluctant even to talk about the fact that we are gods.

Forked Radish, or a "God"?

There is a story about a priest who, entering the sanctuary one morning for a few moments of private worship, stood before the altar. He bowed his head in humility and said, "I am nothing, nothing!" A younger priest entered in time to hear the remark. He, too, bowed his head, and hand on his breast, murmured, "I am nothing, nothing." The janitor had paused in his work a few feet away to listen. He bowed his head and said, somewhat more loudly, "I am nothing, nothing!" The older priest looked up and said, "Look who thinks he's nothing!"

The story has a painful implication: our declaration that we are nothing, that we are mere sinful human beings, smacks of pride. He "doth protest too much, me thinks."

The paradox is that in one sense man is merely "a forked radish," as Shakespeare put it, yet one capable of atrocities never seen among animals. Each of us is just one of three and a half billion struggling individuals populating a tiny and insignificant planet off in a corner of a limitless universe.

In another sense man is a god, a fragment of divinity inhabiting a human body. Each of us is caught up in the same paradoxical predicament which the Apostle Paul experienced when he said, "I do not do the good I want, but the evil I do not want is what I do. . . . Wretched man that I am! Who will deliver me from this . . . ?"[2] The knowledge that Jesus accepted fully his humanity and completely accepted his divinity tells us that this is the goal, and that in some degree it is possible for anyone.

I like the freedom God gives us, but I fear the terrible responsibility. I would not want him to deprive me of my freedom, but—once in a while, when things get too rough—I'd like for him to take over just a little, especially where other people are concerned and obviously wrong, and in need of punishment or correction. Thus speaks the inner child who wants to be free, but refuses to accept full responsibility. So speaks the hippie who wants to be free of all restraints, but demands that parents or society subsidize him in his idleness.

Even an unlimited monarch is restricted to the boundaries of his own kingdom. He cannot, except by invasion or intrigue or persuasion, exercise control over an adjoining kingdom. Our autonomy, too, is limited. There are other people whose rights we must respect. There are penalties imposed if we do not.

"The kingdom of God is within you," Jesus said.[3] Yes, but how, where, and what is it? How do I get in touch with it? One translation tries to solve the apparent mystery by having it read, "the kingdom of God is among you."[4] For me this solves nothing, explains nothing.

I would paraphrase the statement like this: "The kingdom of heaven, of God, is within you, and you are the absolute monarch of that kingdom. You have been entrusted with a portion of divinity. It is the uncreated self, your God-self. As king of that inner realm you are in charge, responsible only to God in whose image you are made."

There are other limitations, imposed by one's genetic wiring and environmental conditioning. For instance, I am reasonably sure I could never become a mathematician, a nuclear physicist, or a concert pianist. Nor can I fly by waving my arms, a limitation imposed by physical laws. However, within the framework of my selfhood, I am in charge. I am responsible for what becomes of me, for what I do to others, and for my ultimate destiny.

You Decide What Is Right

A young woman came to me for counseling. Hers was a very sick marriage, and she was undecided as to whether to end it, or try to patch it up. I said, "I will have no advice to offer you, nor any pat solutions. I will simply help you

31

discover at the center of your nature what you must do, and then help you do it."

It seemed obvious to me that she had married for totally neurotic reasons, and that the marriage had no chance of enduring, but I maintained an impartial attitude.

After some months she said emphatically, "I now see that it is a sick marriage because I married for very, very sick reasons. It can never succeed. I want out!" I then sought to show her what a rough road she would travel if she dissolved the marriage, but she was adamant. She had seen the truth, and, I think, quite properly abandoned a relationship which should never have been entered into. She accepted responsibility for her own actions, and at no point did she ask my advice as to what decision she should make.

Every psychologist, minister, or psychiatrist, however, discovers that the true neurotic will demand to be told what he ought to do. He wants decisions made for him, and refuses to accept responsibility.

Christ did not tell his hearers that they must believe any particular set of doctrines. He did not tell them what to believe at all, except when he said, "You believe in God, believe also in me."[5] This was more of an invitation than a command. He did not encourage them to rely upon outward laws and guides. In fact he said to the Pharisees, "Why can't you decide for yourselves what is right?"[6] They relied exclusively upon the law of Moses and their own innumerable additions to it. They kept the law meticulously as their final, ultimate authority. Now Jesus astounds them—and us—by asking why they did not decide in their own hearts what was right or wrong.

Obviously this cannot be applied to children, the immature, or those ignorant of the basic laws of God and man. But once we have mastered the fundamental teachings of Christ, for instance, we do not need to refer to the sixth chapter of Matthew to discover what Jesus' attitude was toward forgiveness. Nor, approaching a curb painted red, do we need to pull out a vehicle code manual to learn the significance of the red curb. After we have been driving awhile, we know what red curbs mean. Once we are acquainted with the basic teachings of Jesus, we should, if reasonably mature spiritually, be able to decide within ourselves what is right.

Robert Browning said much the same thing in his poem *Paracelsus*:

> Truth is within ourselves; it takes no rise
> From outward things, whate'er you may believe.
> There is an inmost centre in us all,
> Where truth abides in fulness; and around,
> Wall upon wall, the gross flesh hems it in,
> This perfect, clear perception—which is truth.
> A baffling and perverting carnal mesh
> Binds it, and makes all error: and to KNOW
> Rather consists in opening out a way
> Whence the imprisoned splendour may escape,
> Than in effecting entry for a light
> Supposed to be without.[7]

This inner light is Christ. "I am the light of the world," he said.[8] Having seen in him what true humanity is, and perceived in him true divinity, we commit ourselves to him. In committing all of ourselves that we can, to all of Christ we understand, we take the first firm step toward "effecting entry for a light," as Browning put it. We are then no longer bound by laws, traditions, creeds, or dogmas, but released to "walk in the light, as he is in the light."[9] "If the Son makes you free, you will be free indeed."[10]

The struggle is, first, to accept our humanity *and* our divinity, and to merge them. Thus the two warring selves are at last united. The second step is to commit this united self to Christ, the Light. But what a struggle it can be to abandon oneself to the will of God! "What if I were to end up as a missionary in Outer Mongolia?" one man asked. Someone replied, "If you did, you'd be far happier there than you are right now."

Most people want no interference from God except in a crisis. The rest of the time they would much prefer to go it alone. Paradoxically, God wants us to be responsible for our actions, yet be willing to listen to the inner Voice which is offering guidance.

Whenever I am on a plane approaching the airport, I always earnestly hope that the pilot is willing and anxious to listen to instructions from the tower. In calling the tower for instructions the pilot does not limit his autonomy. His survival and that of his passengers depends upon his complete and perfect obedience to instructions. Thus, planes land and take off at a busy airport every sixty seconds or oftener and fly at predetermined altitudes, all under the control of someone in the control tower. Directions and commands issuing from the tower do not in any sense limit the freedom of the pilot. He is free to ignore them, but he will do so at the risk of disaster.

The commandments of Jesus are not an effort to infringe upon our autonomy, but rather to make certain that our lives will be more harmonious. As kings of our own inner kingdom, our welfare and happiness and fulfillment hinge upon how well we obey these fundamental principles Jesus has given us. He is the "control tower," but will not coerce us.

A Sense of Identity

A lovely young married woman had been struggling for years with an obsession neurosis. Obsessive thoughts would come to her unbidden, and repeat themselves endlessly. Some of the thoughts dealt with doing severe bodily harm to her children. Others had to do with sex, and some seemed more like "mental debris," but once an unwanted thought entered her mind she could not eradicate it. In addition she had a large number of compulsions—things she felt compelled to do whether they made sense or not. Psychiatrists had attempted all of the usual procedures, including tranquilizers. She was still miserable.

In counseling sessions with her, and later in a Yokefellow group, she began to discover the roots of her problem. She had little sense of personal worth. She did not really know who she was as a person. To compensate for her sense of inferiority, which had originated in childhood, she developed a "princess syndrome." She felt that she had to be first in everything, the most loved, the most adored. This, of course, is a neurotic need to compensate for a lack of true identity.

It took her approximately thirty years to become that sort of person, and eradicating the symptoms—through building a true identity—did not come overnight. But gradually, through her group experience, she began to discard the hurt little-girl voice and mannerisms. Genuine growth of an identity became apparent. She came to see herself not as "special," but unique, as one of three and a half billion people, yet loved of God as much as anyone else on earth.

In the desert Moses received the command to return to Egypt and lead his people out of bondage. He asked, "Who am I . . . ?" Who am I that I should be the one chosen for this important task?[11] He did not receive an immediate answer to his question, but his answer came through the succeeding years in obedience to God. He discovered his true identity as he sought to discover and do the will of God. Our true identity unfolds as we seek to discover the glorious will of God, and get into harmony with it.

We derive a sense of identity early in life, or fail to, depending upon our environment. If parents are punitive and judgmental and life is harsh, if demands are made upon the child which cannot at the moment be met, a sense of helplessness envelops him. He may feel defeated, worthless and vaguely guilty.

Ellen was such a person. She was married and in her thirties. For over a year, an hour each weeek, we sought out the roots of her confusion about herself and her identity. Tyrannical parents had crushed her spirit. A moralistic and judgmental religion had made her fearful of God. She felt "bad," helpless under the lash of her mother's indignant demands. The mother of several children, she felt more their age emotionally than a woman in her thirties.

A year or more of previous psychiatric probing had revealed only that she had a "sex hangup," but she didn't know what to do about it. Her religious and home environment had made sex a "no-no," yet she sensed there was something wrong with her basic attitudes.

For a year in counseling sessions we dealt with this basic block in her emotional and spiritual nature, and she finally came to feel, as well as understand intellectually, that all which God has made is good. At that point I put her in a Yokefellow group of eight or ten individuals. The damage done to her in early childhood was not easily eradicated, but she persisted, until, little by little, she came to have a sense of identity and the ability to stand up to her overbearing mother. She learned how to say "yes" to God and life, and "no" to unreasonable demands of those who sought to control her. She became a "person," in that she gained a sense of worth. Her false guilt, based upon warped religious teachings early in childhood, gave way to a sense of release as she came to accept the God-self within.

One's sense of identity can be lost, too, in a number of ways. A woman may lose it by being beaten down, criticized and berated. In time she may come to suspect that she is as stupid as her parents or husband maintain, or as selfish, or egotistical. If a woman fails to achieve a satisfactory marriage relationship, or is not fulfilled as wife and mother, she may to some degree lose her sense of identity. The same thing can happen to anyone, though perhaps women tend to lose their sense of identity more easily.

Depending on how much "ego strength" he achieves early in life, a man may lose some of his sense of identity through repeated failure. Charles was an only child of intelligent parents, but some combination of circumstances had produced a young man who seemed utterly incapable of coping with life. He had a good mind, but his chief interest was in guns, and in the Civil War. He might have become a history teacher, but he lacked sufficient educational background. This gay, charming, somewhat effeminate man was utterly helpless when it came to practical matters, either mechanical, financial, or personal. He simply could not make a living, and began to drink to excess.

Charles eventually took his own life, leaving a note in which he said that he had been a failure as a man, a poor son, an inadequate citizen, and an utter failure as a Christian.

I loved Charles and was saddened by his death. He had never achieved anything of value or significance in life. He could not even earn a living. Having lost confidence in himself, he no longer had any sense of worth, thus no feeling that "I am a worthwhile person." Having no self-worth, he felt no true identity.

There is another way in which one can lose his sense of identity. Simply put, it is through loss of integrity. The Bible calls it sin. Loss of integrity and loss of indentity are much the same. One who becomes a pathological liar can no longer distinguish truth from falsehood. Immorality—the violation of mankind's basic moral codes—produces a loss of identity, in that one no longer has integrity. He is not integrated, whole. He is morally disintegrated. He has dissipated his selfhood. One who willfully violates the basic laws of God has pitted himself against Universal Mind, Divine Consciousness, the Cosmic Forces through which God operates his universe. Such a person is out of harmony with reality, and either destroys himself or is destroyed by the consequences of his own actions.

Who am I? I am a god encapsulated in a temple called a human body. I am responsible to act like a god, and I wince as I write the words, yet it is so. If I fail to act in harmony with the basic universal principles given by Christ, in some way I lose my selfhood.

A poll revealed that 91 percent of all Americans admit that they would have gone to jail if all of their misdeeds had been discovered. Seven million or more Americans are in trouble with the law each year, and the rate is rising rapidly. Only 3 percent of individuals who commit crimes ever go to prison. Forty percent of all boys now living will be arrested during their lifetime for some crime other than traffic violation. Over two hundred murders a week are committed in the United States. Murders and deaths due to traffic accidents are far greater than deaths due to war. Most criminals arrested are in the 15–16 age group. There are nearly one million prisoners on parole today, and nearly half a million in prison.

How Responsible Am I? And for What?

As a god, I am responsible. The words, "Have dominion over the earth" were spoken to each of us at birth. You and I are in charge. We and our ancestors have not done too well.

Our slums and ghettos attest to our human incapacity to accept responsibility. A third of the world's population is starving, and another third ill-fed. Everyone is familar with the fact that earth's three-billion population will become six billion by or before the year 2020 A.D.

Half of all the hospital beds in the U. S. are filled with mental patients. These are not people who have "something wrong with their brains"; they were damaged by their environment, or their own actions.

Why doesn't God do something?

A friend and I were driving to lunch at our favorite eating place, the Golden Lamp Coffeehouse, operated by Yokefellows, Inc., in Burlingame, California. We listened to a news report of some disaster, and we began a discussion of the world's ills—war, poverty, racial discrimination, and all the rest. We were still discussing it when we sat down to order lunch.

I often use my friend as a listening post when I need to blow off steam, and he knows me well enough not to take too seriously anything I may say at such a time. He was calmly studying the menu when I said, "You know, I could design a better world than this on the back of an envelope with the stub of a pencil!"

No sooner had I ended the sentence than I laughed, for instantly a clear, gentle, inner voice asked, "Why don't you?" It was not audible to my friend, of course, but it was to me. I told him and he smiled. "Got your answer?" he asked.

The voice was nonjudgmental, uncritical. It sounded about the way I would expect Christ to speak. In it there seemed to be combined an answer, an ever-so-kind rebuke, and a gentle urge to try to make it a better world.

I recall one night that my son came to me and asked for the keys to the car. He had just gotten his driver's license. Although he had been driving on back roads for practice, with some driving on the main highways, I had observed one or two habits which I felt could cause him trouble. I had two alternatives. I could insist on more practice, or I could hand him the keys. I had pointed out the problem in his driving, but had gotten little or no response—high school students are not noted for a willingness to listen to parents' advice. That night I gave him the keys—and prayed to the effect that if or when he had an accident he wouldn't hurt anyone else or himself. He did have an accident some months later, but no one was injured. After that he became a very cautious driver.

I wonder if God must have felt some qualms when he turned the Garden over to Adam and Eve, with one final warning. They were in charge. Run it. He would be around. In fact Adam had daily communion with him. Then it happened.

Adam, you recall, blamed his wife. She blamed the serpent. Evicted from Paradise, they must have engaged in recrimination as to whose fault it was. Children hear more than we imagine. They learn more from what they see and hear than from what we tell them. Thus, their sons Cain and Abel had an altercation, and as a result the first murder took place.

God's only other alternative was to make man a robot, a mechanical man, or an overly compliant individual virtually incapable of choosing. But, because he is who he is, his children had to be made in his image—free to choose.

No, we have not done a very commendable job in "having dominion" over the earth. Man has failed in a thousand ways. But no one of us is responsible for the world's problems. We are responsible only for the inner kingdom of Self. To the degree that I can bring my God-self into harmony with the will of the Father, my own kingdom will be a harmonious one. "As many as are led by the spirit of God, they are the sons of God."[12] That is, God's true children will be guided by him. When this happens, all of our relationships and activities will be under his direction. This is all he asks.

Some of the worst things that ever happened to me proved in the long run to have been blessings. I needed, desperately, the discipline of hardship as a young man. The Apostle Paul wrote, concerning the disasters which had befallen him, that "what has happened to me has really served to advance the gospel."[13] The thirteenth chapter of 1 Corinthians, the love chapter, was written to help settle a quarrel in the church of Corinth. God does not intend our sorrows, but he can use them and weave them into the fabric of life.

Alfred Adler, an early disciple of Freud, believed that the urge to achieve, to compensate for one's inferiority feelings, is man's strongest drive. History is replete with accounts of men and women who overcame handicaps and were spurred to achievement by some galling weakness or handicap. Another eminent psychiatrist has suggested that a certain excessiveness seems essential to significant achievement. A too well-balanced personality, he said, seems often almost on *dead* center. Handicaps, hardship, provide challenges which act—at least for some—as a powerful drive.

Unfortunately, millions of other are crushed by the oppressive weight of poverty, ignorance, and other forces too great for them to handle. It is they to whom we owe an obligation. They are "the least of these," and Jesus sternly charged his listeners that they were not to despise or ignore these. We are in charge; we are responsible for our world. Collectively we are responsible to God for what happens in the ghetto, to the underprivileged, the despised and rejected, the alcoholic, the moral derelict, the convict, the dope pusher and his victims. Man is responsible for war and drunken driving, for disease and suffering, since all of this came about through man's rebellion against God. And I am Man.

Individually I am not responsible for the totality of mankind's suffering. I am not my brother's keeper, and it is not stated in the Bible that I am supposed to be. I am to be my brother's *brother,* for he and I are children of the same Father. As his brother I am responsible to act in love toward him.

You are in charge of your own life, responsible to make of it what you can.

You are the king of your own personal kingdom; and it is the will of the Father, after you have set your own kingdom in order, that you reach out and embrace all whom you can. It can be a word, a gesture, a touch, encouragement, love. How can you know what to do or say? "If anyone wants to do God's will, he will know. . . ."[14] "If we walk in the light, as he is in the light, we have fellowship with one another. . . ."[15] This fellowship was meant to be a healing, redemptive one, in which God's love is channeled through us to others.

3.

How You Can Receive
Forgiveness

> "Our sins do not cause Him to love us less; and no amount of good we do wins from Him any greater love or forgiveness."
>
> —GERMAINE ST. CLOUD

I ONCE said in a sermon that, after repenting, "thirty minutes is long enough for a person to feel guilty about anything." Elaborating upon this, I pointed out that there is nothing in the Bible which urges us to wallow in remorse and guilt. We are not commanded to condemn and hate ourselves for our mistakes and blunders, but to recognize our sins, confess them, and receive forgiveness.

There is no virtue in berating ourselves day after day, year after year, for our spiritual or moral blunders. "Stir filth this way or that, it is still filth," as the Jewish mystic, Isaac of Meir, has put it. Repent (meaning to turn from it), be done with it, and move on, resolving to do better.

After the service a very angry woman berated me for what I had said. She had, with her selective hearing, turned out much of what I had said, and interpreted my statement as implying a blanket license to sin. I do not recall that she ever spoke to me again.

I am not suggesting "easy grace," or a light-hearted approach to the problem of evil. On the contrary, guilt is the most destructive of all emotions, and must be dealt with appropriately. In general I find that most people tend to fall into two equally disastrous categories: either they wallow in guilt, and cannot forgive themselves; or else they consider their sins and mistakes of no significance. A rather small proportion of Christians seems able to deal with sin and guilt in a creative way.

Join the Human Race

A young minister's wife, riddled with anxiety stemming from unresolved guilt, belonged to a Yokefellow group which consisted of about ten persons meeting weekly. I happened to be the leader and observed her emotional and spiritual growth during the several years she attended the group. Hers was largely false guilt, based on generalized feelings of inadequacy, rejection in childhood, and inability to feel acceptable to God, herself, or her husbnad. All of these emotions register on the unconscious mind as guilt. She could not distinguish at first between real and false guilt. Her self-rejection, frustration, inability to love, and guilt over perfectly normal emotions, were damaging her and all of her relationships.

In the group, which dealt with emotions and relationships rather than theological concepts, she felt free to express her true feelings for the first time. Ocassionally she expressed hostility, about which she had always felt guilty. She found acceptance in the group, much to her surprise

One evening she said, "I've just decided to join the human race and admit that I'm a sinner, and so what! Isn't that what it's all about—to admit it, confess it, and let God forgive us?" Though the truth of her statement seems quite obvious, it represented a genuine breakthrough for her. She had stopped trying to be perfect! The little girl in her, who had always sought to please and placate in order to win approval, now decided to give way to the adult self and admit to being human. We could perceive genuine growth in her from that moment.

She was sensing at a feeling level what we all know intellectually, and what the Bible makes quite clear: that we are all sinners, that God knows about it, and is anxious to forgive us. Though we know all this in our heads, it is quite another thing to bridge the gap between our humanity and our divinity, to accept both our frailties and failures, while seeking to measure up to the divinity within us which urges us toward some distant goal of perfection.

The young woman had attended church and Sunday school all of her life, but only in a small group had she been able to learn self-forgiveness, and accept fully the forgiveness of God. It became possible for her when she discovered in the loving group an acceptance of her just as she was—faults and all. Her occasional bursts of anger were accepted, and she came to learn at a feeling level that anger is not necessarily evil. She learned how to give and accept love, affection, and tenderness. Her fear of, and hostility toward men, gradually diminished. In the process she began to accept herself as a woman, and as a child of God who was forgiven and accepted.

Having devoted over forty years to the ministry, I feel the need neither to defend nor to criticize the church. But it is obvious that in its present form—which I am sure bears little resemblance to the early church—it is not equipped to meet the personal, individual needs of a great many people. One hour a week spent in worship (and only about 40 percent of church members are in church on any given Sunday) was never intended to meet all of our spiritual and emotional needs.

A university freshman, filling out a form the first day at school, came to the question: "What are your personal strengths?" He pondered this for a moment, then wrote: "Sometimes I am trustworthy, loyal, helpful, friendly, kind, courteous, brave, obedient, cheerful, thrifty, clean and reverent." The next question was: "What are your chief weaknesses?" He wrote: "Sometimes I am *not* trustworthy, loyal, helpful, friendly, kind, courteous, brave, obedient, cheerful, thrifty, clean and reverent." His problem is one that confronts us all. Sometimes we act like Christians, and sometimes we don't. As humans we are caught up in the eternal problem of good and evil, right and wrong, sin and salvation, guilt and grace. The animal and the angel within are in conflict.

We crucify ourselves between two thieves: remorse over the past, and anxiety concerning the future. This, then, is the human dilemma: the problem of fear and faith, guilt and grace, sin and forgiveness.

As if to compound our problem there are some statements in the Bible which, as children, many people misunderstood. I recall a splendid Christian woman who rather hesitantly asked me in a counseling session about the statement of one of the psalms, "In sin did my mother conceive me."[1] This had troubled her for many years, for it seemed to equate conception (and thus human sexuality) with sin. I explained that the psalmist was simply expressing in exaggerated poetic imagery his feeling that he had been a sinner from the moment he was conceived; and that this did not in any sense suggest that sexuality, conception, and birth were sinful.

Apparently she had many lifelong misconceptions about sexuality, for she then posed the question: "Didn't the sin of Adam and Eve relate to sexual relations? Wasn't that what the apple symbolized?" I pointed out that Genesis makes no reference to an apple, but refers only to fruit. (She was sure I was wrong, and went home to look it up.) I also reminded her that God had said to Adam and Eve, "Be fruitful and multiply, and replenish the earth." This gave her great relief, for she had simply blotted that part of the story from memory.

Fortunately not everyone has been as badly misinformed about our God-given sexuality, but the sex drive is still the source of much guilt, both real and false, for many people.

Guilt Over Our Two Strongest Emotions

It seems ironic that guilt should be the most damaging of all emotions, and that in our culture the God-implanted emotions of sex and anger seem to produce the greatest amount of guilt. These two drives, aggression and the love-sex emotion, are the strongest we have; and thus society has surrounded anger and sexual expression with numerous prohibitions and controls. Uncontrolled anger is destructive to society. It requires restraints and controls, both from within and without. Sexual expression, thought by Freud to be our strongest drive, can create havoc in any society unless it is channeled and controlled.

From earliest infancy the child is taught to control his anger. He learns that it displeases mother if he hits or bites someone, or goes into a screaming rage. He is usually punished, if not physically, at least by mother's rejection. If he is never permitted to express any negative emotion, his anger goes underground and will express itself later in physical or emotional symptoms, or in antisocial conduct.

Long before the child is even faintly aware of the differences between the sexes, he discovers his body. If parents feel there is something inherently indecent about the human body or sex, the child will pick this up on his infant radar, and a neurotic sense of guilt is in the making. When a child is punished for normal curiosity about sex, the message is imparted that human sexuality is something indecent, or wrong, or bad.

I recall visiting a psychotic young woman in a mental institution who believed that she had committed the unforgivable sin. Her "sin" was thinking about sex, which she equated with sin. It is tragic to discover how many lives have been warped by such misconceptions. In a Midwestern city where I was conducting a retreat a husband and wife asked for a counseling session. They dealt with some relatively unimportant issues, and as the hour was coming to a close, the husband rather casually said, "Well, the truth of the matter is I'm a bastard and always will be." He said it in a semi-facetious vein, but something in his face prompted me to ask, "Why do you feel that you are a bastard?"

"Because I am. I was an illegitimate child."

"And this has troubled you all these years?"

"It sure has. I've always felt worthless; and why shouldn't I, being a bastard?"

I said, "My friend, you have been the victim of a tragic misconception. *You* are not illegitimate. Your *parents* were, in that it was not legitimate for them to bring a child into the world unless they were married. But you were born just as God meant for you to be—in a perfectly normal way! There's nothing wrong with *you*. Any shame or guilt belongs to your father and mother."

He sat stunned. "You mean I'm okay? I'm not worthless or guilty?"

"Of course not!"

A slow smile began to spread over his face, and he looked at his wife with amazement and wonder and release. She smiled and said, "Honey, I'm so glad you've gotten this thing all straightened out in your mind. It's held you back all your life."

This was an instance of the destructive power of false

45

guilt. The man had taken to himself the guilt of his father and mother, and it had made him less a person because of his misconception.

Many of our guilt areas have been repressed into the unconscious mind. A woman who had attended a one-day retreat which I conducted at her church wrote as follows:

Yokefellows, Inc.
209 Park Road
Burlingame, California 94010

Gentlemen:

Rev. Glenn Miller brought the Yokefellow program to our church several years ago. I hobbled into the meeting on my crutches just in time to hear Dr. Osborne say, "Repressed resentment is one major cause of rheumatoid arthritis."

It was as if he had thrown a bomb into my lap! The doctors had said I would never get any better. When Dr. Osborne made that statement, I knew immediately that I had repressed my resentment of my father, although my mother and I had often mentioned how fortunate it was that I *had* been able to forgive. But now I knew I had never forgiven him fully.

I attended the Yokefellow group for many months and learned how to deal with each phase of my "renewal." I had to learn many things. (1) I had to admit that "as a man thinketh in his heart so is he." (2) I had to forgive my father. (3) I had, finally, to forgive myself. (4) The hate had to be replaced with understanding and love. I learned so much about the real "me."

Eventually I graduated to a cane and then began to walk without a cane. I thank God for the opportunity to be a Yokefellow! It has brought me new life.

Sincerely,

Mary Jane Switzler

How easy it is to deceive ourselves! Mary Jane had convinced herself that she had forgiven her father, but her inner self knew the truth, and when she could admit it, she took the long slow road toward honesty with herself and with God. Spiritual and physical healing resulted. No amount of earnest prayer for healing would have helped her, for the mind and spirit often hand their conflict over to the body, and physical illness results. *Honesty with oneself, with God, and with others is the first all-essential step toward spiritual and physical well-being.*

Growth, the Meaning of Life

Something in us urges us upward. It is the part of us that aspires to do more, be more, achieve more, love more, to grow emotionally and spiritually. I believe that this "upward reach of the soul" is not encapsulated in that portion of us designated as "the spirit," but that this growth principle resides in every cell and atom and molecule in every living thing. For growth is the meaning of life, and whatever makes for growth is good. Anything which limits growth is evil.

An English woman living in a foreign country chided a bus driver one day because the bus was never on time. "Why don't you make an effort to keep to a schedule?" she said.

"But Madam, that is impossible!"

"Of course not. In England the buses run on time. If only you'd try a little harder you could do it, and that would be perfect."

"Perfect!" He looked aghast. "Perfection is for God. We are but humans!"

The bus driver's reaction is the problem all of us face. If we set our standards too high, we can become neurotically guilt-laden, hating ourselves for failure to attain the goal. If we set them too low, we fail to measure up to our true potential. How shall we resolve the problem? In a sense the question is rhetorical, because the superego (roughly equivalent to conscience) is formed by early environmental factors, chiefly mother and father and other authority figures. Whether one has a neurotically demanding, condemnatory conscience, or ends up at the other extreme with little or no moral sense, is usually determined long before the child has reached his teens.

Does this mean that we have no responsibility? On the contrary, we are still responsible. We are *not* accountable for what was done to us by our parents, or other factors; but we *are* held responsible to become our highest and best under the circumstances. Jesus gave us the formula in his statement, "To whom much is given, of him will much be required."[2] Conversely, God expects less of those whose

47

opportunity or advantages were minimal. Whatever our limitations, or endowments, we are in charge of our own lives and destiny, and we need to keep growing.

In a Yokefellow group session involving eight or ten persons, a young married woman finally shared some of her deeper feelings one evening. She was fairly new to the group and had not opened up to any great degree. She appeared cultured and poised, but quite reticent. Finally I said, "Jane, I pick up a kind of longstanding sadness in your voice. It's as old as you are. Something happened back there that hurt you very deeply. Could you tell us about it?" Her lifelong protective barriers were still in place as in a rather flat voice she told a little of her tragic childhood. There was love and understanding in the group, and a feeling that she needed desperately to deal with some old and painful memories.

As she told of her early childhood, she began to cry almost uncontrollably. A woman sitting beside her put her arm around her and held her like a child. Finally the young woman was able, through her tears, to get out some of her story.

She had been reared in direst poverty, and permitted to grow up like a wild animal by parents who had nothing to give in terms of love or culture or material things. She was twelve before she was ever in a home with an inside toilet. That was when she was sent by the welfare agency to live with a family some distance away. It proved to be a terrible experience. They wanted to give her love, and expected her to love them; but she did not know what love was and could neither give nor receive it.

"I didn't know how to act," she said. "They tried to teach me, and I was so scared I couldn't learn anything. I was miserable and just wanted to go back to the hovel that was home. The welfare people finally took me back home. I was happier there, but I was still just a dirty, ignorant little animal."

An older sister had somehow managed to break out of that limited environment. She had gotten an education and married. She sent for the younger girl and determined to make something of her. It was a fiasco from the start. And yet, the frightened little girl with the matted hair who had fought off all efforts to civilize her had somehow become the cultured, poised, pretty young wife who was telling us the story of her life.

She still did not know how to give or receive love, and was experiencing difficulty in her marriage. After she had concluded her story the group stood in the center of the room in a tight circle. Jane was put in the center and held, lovingly, by the entire group. Several of the women were crying—two in particular whose own home background had marred them. It was a genuine circle of love. There was prayer—a heartfelt expression of gratitude for what this lovely young woman had done with her life to that point. The group asked God's help and guidance for her in the future. An atmosphere of love pervaded the room.

Jane was absent the following week. I phoned to tell her that we had missed her. She said, "I felt I was being criticized for what I had said." I was aghast.

"But Jane, no one voiced any criticism. Nothing was expressed but love and acceptance and understanding. Couldn't you feel it in the woman who held you as you wept and as the group surrounded you with their love?"

"No, I couldn't feel a thing but that I was wrong or guilty or unworthy. But I'll come back. I'm glad you called. I wasn't sure just how the group reacted to me."

Jane did return to the group, to learn how to give and receive love—wanting, needing, but fearing it. She was not responsible for the damage done to her, but saw that she alone was in charge of her destiny. She accepted that responsibility.

I am certain that God expects much more of me than he does of Jane. Just how much more I am not sure. Jane has no idea at this moment what God and life expect of her; but she is determined with God's help, manifested partly through her Yokefellow group, to become a worthwhile person.

The Two Aspects of Forgiveness

There are two kinds of judgment which we experience. The first is how we perceive God—as either loving, forgiving, and accepting, or as punitive and judgmental. Then there is the inner judicial system. If one has a condemning conscience, he finds it hard to forgive himself, though he may know intellectually that God has forgiven him. Thus, in a sense, there are two aspects to forgiveness; the divine forgiveness of God and our own self-forgiveness. I am convinced that there is no genuine sense of "cleansing" until we are able to forgive ourselves. I have known Christians who clung to their guilt twenty, thirty, or forty years without ever getting the sense of release that comes from being able to forgive oneself.

Sin is basically estrangement from God, from others, and from self. When we are thus estranged, we are out of harmony, "out of love" with God, others, and ourselves. We then commit all manner of errors. Any act or attitude that alienates us from God is sin. Whatever makes us feel out of harmony with God or man is sin, no matter what others may think. It is true that one's conscience may be overly strict, in which case it needs to become enlightened so that we will not live under the lash of constant self-condemnation. Some, of course, have an impaired conscience with too weak a moral sense.

Alberta had been reared in an orphanage. She had never known her father, and was abandoned by her mother. She made her own way after leaving the orphanage and managed to hold down a responsible position. Through she was quite attractive, she had not married. I sensed that she desperately needed love but was ambivalent about men. Finally, in her thirties she met a man in his forties who had been divorced three times. They came to me a number of times for counseling, and my own feeling was that the proposed marriage had little chance of success. He was a poor marriage risk on a number of counts, and she needed, feared, and resented men. Of course, she was totally unaware of her ambivalent feelings about men. The marriage lasted a hectic three years. She emerged from the divorce bitter and disillusioned, resolved never to trust another man. In a Yokefellow group which was understanding and accepting, she poured out the full force of her vitriolic hostility toward her ex-husband. He was the only man she had ever loved, and she now hated him. Yet, with a part of her nature she still needed and loved him.

Alberta had always held good positions, but now everything seemed to go wrong. She lost her job, and one evening without consciously intending to, she got drunk and ended up in bed with a man she barely knew. She became pregnant.

When she came to see me Alberta was in panic. She was unemployed, pregnant, frightened, and had to move. Besides, she was virtually without funds. Who could assume the awesome responsibility of trying to judge who had sinned, and how much? Why did her mother abandon her? Who had warped the mother? What kind of treatment did Alberta receive in the orphanage? How much love had she known? All I could feel was compassion and understanding. One honest mistake—marrying the wrong man in search of love—had led to a succession of others. Someone once said that after taking a mouthful of too-hot coffee, anything you do thereafter will be wrong. Sometimes a simple mistake in judgment can lead one into an almost hopeless maze of disasters. It is not a matter of blame or judgment, but rather how to resolve the situation.

Alberta made it. I told her that I would get the man to be responsible for the hospital costs when the baby came, and that I would be her friend. Her relief was infinite that one person in the world cared.

Real and False Guilt

False guilt and real guilt are equally damaging to one's emotional and spiritual nature. I have known men and women who ended up in mental institutions solely as the result of false guilt—inordinate self-condemnation for imaginary sins. But there are also countless men and women, in and out of mental institutions, who suffer from real guilt, or a mixture of real and false guilt.

Real guilt is, at its core, *trying to pursue incompatible goals*. The conflict produces anxiety, which is destructive to the personality. God is "against" sin because it is damaging to the personality, and conceivably to another who may be injured in the process.

Guilt is one thing, and the feeling of guilt is another. There are those with a weak moral sense who are guilty yet feel no guilt. Others, with an overactive or overscrupulous conscience, may experience untold anguish from needless self-condemnation. These people have great difficulty in feeling forgiven by God, or if they do feel his forgiveness, they may be unable to forgive themselves.

There is no single act of forgiveness on the part of God, no "moment" when he decides to pardon us. He has always extended forgiveness to us, for it is a part of his nature. He cannot do otherwise.

51

The father of the prodigal son did not utter any word of forgiveness when the errant son returned. In his eagerness to receive the son back into fellowship he did not even permit him to complete his carefully rehearsed speech of repentance. The son had always been forgiven in his father's mind, for the father was that kind of a person. Yet, the forgiveness could not be experienced, or become operative, until the son returned in repentance and humility.

There was no condemnation on the part of the father, no inquiry as to what he had done with his inheritance, no rebuke for the wasted time spent away from home, no probing into the details of what had transpired, only rejoicing over the fact of his return.

Does God punish? The answer is yes and no. God does not punish, but there are consequences which may *feel* like judgment or punishment. The wandering, disobedient son had experienced some consequences—abandonment by his supposed friends, hunger and privation, and now the humiliation of having to go home and face the music. But the father said no word of condemnation. There was no punishment from the father. With what surprise and wonderment the son discovered that instead of rebuking him the father held a homecoming banquet. The son was given the best robe, and restored to fellowship. He was treated as if it had never happened!

Jesus is telling us in this parable[3] that God is more anxious to extend forgiveness than we are to receive it. His *forgiveness* is involved in, and a part of, his *acceptance*. He simply accepts us *as if we had never sinned*. We speak of the love of God, of his patience, his redemptive nature, and his forgiveness as though these were all separate attributes; but they are all one and the same thing: simply an overwhelming love, and desire to receive us back into fellowship. Because this is the nature of God, he has—by his nature—taken the initiative. The rest is up to us. Whatever transpires will be the result of *our* initiative. We are always in charge of—responsible for—the decision to return in repentance, or to continue to live out of fellowship with the Father.

But there still remains a nagging question: what about the unrepentant sinners, the Hitlers and Stalins of earth; what of the bitter, vidictive, hostile and unloving people? I am quite content to leave this matter in God's hands. It isn't my problem, nor is it yours. But Jesus' description of the final judgment leads us to believe that there is a reckoning, a revealing of the secrets of the hearts of men. The unrepentant, Jesus said, would be "cast . . . into outer darkness," or "depart . . . into everlasting fire."[4] I don't know what that implies, but I don't like the sound of it. Do they get a second chance? One scripture often quoted is, "It is appointed unto men once to die, but after this the judgment."[5] That may or may not answer the question. Fortunately or otherwise we have incomplete answers to many aspects of God's future plans; but these matters need not concern us unduly. We each have enough light for guidance. Who is there who is living up to all of the light he has? This is our sole responsibility.

I was with a group of relatives sailing from Miami to the Bahamas. The skipper and owner of the sixty-five-foot racing vessel asked me to take the wheel one night as we were, crossing the Gulf Stream. My nautical knowledge is limited to a knowledge of fore and aft, port and starboard. I had spent an hour or two at the wheel that afternoon, and halfway mastered the idea of steering in relation to the compass, which always seemed to be revolving in the wrong direction. But that night in an effort to effect some kind of harmony between the wheel and the compass, I managed to steer the ship in a complete circle. I had my eyes glued to the compass, which was revolving in some absurd and incomprehensible manner, when someone said, "I think you're going in circles." So I was. There was no particular condemnation involved, just an observation. Had there been a collision, it would have been a consequence, not a punishment. I corrected course, finally got the hang of the thing again, and managed to do a fairly creditable job thereafter. It had been an honest, bungling mistake. It had been my inept best; thus there was no need for remorse or breastbeating.

If I had piled the boat up on the rocks, I would have felt something else—a mixture of emotions, perhaps; anger that someone had given me more responsibility than I was capable of handling; self-blame for accepting it or for failure to do better.

Another aspect of guilt is revealed when we know what

we should do, are capable of doing it, and refuse. "The man who knows the good he ought to do and does not do it is a sinner."[6] For instance, Jesus taught explicitly that we are to love our enemies, and forgive those who despitefully use us.[7] If I refuse to seek a reconciliation, I am living in sin—deliberately refusing to obey a universal, cosmic principle. It is not that I have angered God, but that I have gotten out of harmony with some immutable spiritual laws. I thus harm myself and others.

We may define real guilt as deliberate refusal to obey a known spiritual principle. We know full well the basic law underlying all others: to love God, one's neighbor, and oneself. On this depends all other laws. To fulfill this, Paul said, fufills all others.[8] Loving God, man, and ourselves we will obey traffic laws, and the multitude of other legal, social, and moral laws set up for the benefit of mankind. To refuse to do this involves genuine guilt.

Just as pain is a beneficent warning signal that something is wrong with the physical organism, guilt is spiritual pain warning that there is something wrong with one's moral and spiritual nature. A toothache warns us that some action needs to be taken. If the tooth is pulled, or properly treated, the pain subsides. Pain has served its benevolent purpose. A feeling of guilt or remorse is a psychic warning signal of some impairment in our spiritual nature. When we have rectified the matter, the guilt feeling should subside. To go on feeling guilty is neurotic.

Wrong Ways to Deal with Guilt

There are many wrong ways to deal with guilt, none of which are successful. Some people indulge in needless self-blame, while others take an equally destructive course and become judgmental of others. They project their own guilt and failure upon those about them. How human it is to try to fix blame, to judge, condemn, to seek to find the guilty party and go after him.

My wife and I once visited a unique and widely known church where, since the church is very heavily endowed, they are endeavoring to minister to a broad cross section of society—hippies, homosexuals, rich, poor, blacks, whites—

and anyone else who wishes to participate. Surely Jesus was interested in such people, for he said, "I did not come to invite virtuous people, but sinners."* Too long the church has been associated with the "upright, uptight" segment of society.

As we entered the large sanctuary, a loud and joyous burst of music engulfed us. The large platform was overflowing with a wildly garbed assortment of young people consisting of choir, orchestra, and others who mingled with the orchestra. The music was thrilling, exciting, joyous, though it was not what one would term "sacred music," whatever that is. I don't know just how one would go about labeling one kind of music "sacred," and another "secular," unless solemnity and sadness be confused with sanctity.

Every seat was taken, and we were surrounded by people of all races and colors, standing and sitting. For the first ten minutes, while the rock band played their joyous music, I was stirred. My wife whispered, "They've already reached me." I felt it, too—a sense of joy and celebration. Later when they sang "The Battle Hymn of the Republic" it was like nothing I had ever heard before—pure joy and ecstasy and victory. They had me, too.

"They have something," I thought. "This is what early Christianity must have been like—a celebration, joyousness." Then a young woman read a bitter, vindictive, hate-filled poem castigating everyone connected with the Establishment. Someone else read a few carefully selected portions of Scripture which sought to point up the poisonous ills of society. Blame was fixed on the evil perpetrators of all mankind's ills.

Then a speaker spent twenty-five minutes or more denouncing the treatment of the Japanese at the outset of the Second World War. (He did not mention Pearl Harbor, the Bataan death march, or Corregidor.) I had already lost the initial sense of celebration and joy. All I could feel now was hate. There was condemnation, judgment, and an expressed determination to take over the corrupt government of city, state and nation.

I began to look around me. Initially I had felt a warm glow of oneness with these joyous people. For the first time I became fully aware that these were largely dropouts from society. I did not object to the wild attire affected by roughly 95 percent of the "worshipers," nor to the beards, or the fact that many seemed unacquainted with soap and water. Then I thought I saw them for what they were: hostile young revolutionaries, unable or unwilling to work for a living, lacking in discipline, antagonistic to the simple virtues of work and regular hours, members of the drug culture of San Francisco. For the last three-fourths of the service, I was completely turned off. What had begun with a sense of joy and soul-stirring music degenerated into hostile blame-fixing.

Then I thought: "The prophets fixed blame and responsibility, too. Perhaps some of this is simply legitimate prophetic preaching, a calling to repentance for the sins of society." I tried to join them in their condemnation of the ills of America, but I couldn't bring it off. Here—as I saw it—were young people who couldn't manage their own lives but who wanted to manage the government. I thought, "Their life style is different from mine. I'm uptight. I belong to the Establishment, and am just feeling threatened by their desire for change. I belong to another generation." And that didn't work either. I kept hearing hate, not love. I saw the vacant stares of scores of young people for whom drug abuse is a way of life.

These inexperienced, youthful, idealistic young people had fallen victim to an almost universal fallacy: the idea that because you can spot an evil, it automatically means that you know how to remedy it. Then I recalled John Kennedy's ironic comment after he had occupied the White House for some months: "I never realized it would be so difficult to change things."

It seemed to me that they had been saying, "It's *their* fault. *They're* all wrong. *Society* is sick. *We* are wise and capable of straightening this out."

Prophetic judgment is one thing. Hostile blame-fixing and irresponsible condemnation of society is another. God knows, and we all know, that our world is very sick. I doubt, however, if an answer is likely to come from the dropouts and drug addicts of San Francisco, who appear to be considerably sicker than the rest of society.

I take a dim view of hostile pacifists, angry proponents of love, people who cannot or will not earn a living but who hand out simplistic blueprints to cure the ills of so-

56

ciety. Civilization has been through endless crises for some thousands of years, and we may as well learn to accept some of our human frailty with tolerance, meanwhile trying to avoid judging the judgers too harshly!

Another unsuccessful method of handling guilt is illustrated by a woman who hobbled into the room and fell into a chair for her first counseling session. She had a number of physical ailments which kept her in bed most of the time. In our first session I asked her to write out for her next visit a list of every feeling and experience related to inferiority, shame, failure, rejection, and guilt.

At the second session, she admitted that she had not found time to write much. What little she had written bore no relationship to the topics I had assigned her. I asked her to sit in a reclining chair, and to close her eyes. I spent several minutes getting her completely relaxed. Then I played a tape recording of some music carefully selected for the purpose. She was quite rigid during the entire time.

When I stopped the music and asked her to sit up, she said, with tears and deep emotion, "It was that abortion twenty years ago. I knew from the first note of that music. It has bothered me all these years, and I never dared tell anyone. I felt so guilty . . ."

Without going into the matter of whether her guilt was real or false, I told her that since she felt guilty about it, we were going to spend some time in learning to accept God's forgiveness. While she relaxed again, I quoted a dozen promises concerning divine forgiveness, and then emphatically affirmed that God had forgiven and accepted her. It took some time, for she had labored under the burden of guilt for twenty years.

Her physical symptoms, of course, bore a relationship to her unresolved guilt. Unconsciously she had been punishing herself with various forms of illness in an effort to atone for her guilt feelings. In subsequent sessions there was ample evidence that her physical disabilities, while painful and by now real and organic, were not irreversible. She began to feel worthy to accept forgiveness, and with it good health. In so doing she was accepting the responsibility of living in harmony with divine law. She came to acknowledge that she is in charge.

There is a picture which I have always loved, though it is hardly great art. I saw it first in a Sunday school room. Because some aspects of the painting seemed overly "pretty," I asked my wife to do an altered copy for me. She did so, and I hung it in my office. It has deep meaning for me.

A smiling Christ is seated, surrounded by several children in modern attire. One little girl is seated on his lap holding his hand and pointing to his palm. The caption is: "What happened to your hand?"

It is just the sort of question a child might ask. In answer one's mind follows the footsteps of Jesus across Galilee and Judea, through the streets of Jerusalem, up the slope to Calvary, where stood those three crosses. On the central one hangs a Man unlike any other who ever walked the earth.

There on a lonely hill was enacted the drama of divine love beyond the power of words to explain: the humility of God who lets us do with him as we will; the tragedy of human perfection being judged by gross and selfish men, convinced that they were doing the will of God. And uneasily we sense that those who rejected Christ were vaguely like us. His selflessness sat in quiet judgment upon their selfishness. His teachings ran counter to their traditional values. He made trouble. Some of the things he taught seemed impractical and difficult to obey. He got in their way by challenging their traditions.

The passive and indifferent ignored him. The activists crucified him, but all were equally guilty of rejecting the Son of God. His best friends and followers deserted him; but after the resurrection when Jesus had gathered his scattered little flock, there was no word of condemnation or criticism for their failure.

Here in microcosm is revealed something of the gentle persuasiveness of Christ—no blame or criticism, but an invitation to love and to commitment. What is there in man, what perversity of spirit, what lurking evil, which prevents him from loving and following such a person as Jesus? Whatever the source of this primeval depravity, God seems to understand, and loves us still.

Francis Thompson, the brilliant, weak mystic who became a drug addict, wrote these lines in *The Hound of Heaven:*

> Halts by me that footfall—
> Is my gloom, after all,
> Shade of His hand, outstretched caressingly?

4.

What a Great Time to Be Alive!

"Haste delays the things of God."
—MEISTER ECKHART

A MAN related recently that his dog's main occupation is that of preventing planes from landing in his backyard. The dog's owner lives fairly near an airport, and planes taking off or landing fly over his home. From the moment the dog hears a plane, he rushes to the fence barking, then follows the plane's flight with intense zeal and frantic barking as it disappears in the distance. Then, tail wagging, eyes alight with the joy of a deed well done, he sits down quite pleased with himself, awaiting his master's praise. He has averted another catastrophe!

If one were to assess the world's current situation solely from newspaper headlines, he could easily become as agitated as the dog who saw in every plane an impending disaster.

Before we throw up our hands in resignation, or frantically join another half-dozen societies to solve the world's ills and avert certain doom, it may be well to take a long look at history.

One Roman emperor, who reigned around the time of Christ, ordered four hundred slaves and all of their families killed because one of them had slain an official of his. Another Roman emperor crucified three thousand Jews because of a rebellion.

Going back somewhat farther into history, the Canaanites worshiped the fire-god, Moloch, to whom they sacrificed their living infants. One historian calls theirs the "Nastiest religion in history." The Phoenicians sacrificed the first-born of every animal, and the first-born infant in every family to their god to appease his wrath.

Half a hundred conquerors swept over the Mediterranean world and left uncounted millions of corpses in their wake. Genghis Khan and Attila the Hun were outdone in their insane destruction of cities and empires by at least two other conquerors who ravaged the land, leaving no living thing in their path.

History Repeats Itself

A statesman said: "Politicians have strained their ingenuity to discover new sources of revenue. They have broadened perilously the field of income and property tax. When I was a boy, wealth was regarded as secure and admirable, but now a man has to defend himself for being rich as if it were a crime." The speaker was Socrates, who lived roughly four hundred years before Christ.

Another quotation is pertinent: "These are indeed perilous times. Our young people are rebelling against established authority. They are indifferent to convention and are no longer neat in appearance. They are openly disobedient to their parents. If they are to become our future leaders, there is indeed little hope for the world." This is Socrates again, as he viewed the scene in ancient Greece.

Dr. Nathan Adler, a prominent psychologist teaching at the University of California at Berkeley where all manner of youthful dissent, rebellion, and anarchy have been the vogue said:

They were long-haired and young, and wore wild, bright-colored clothing. Sometimes they frolicked nude in the streets, chanted obscenities at their elders—and consumed generous amounts of dope. Reared during an age of doomsday-oriented crises, they were protesting the growing, rampant materialism of their parents' generation.

This sounds familiar, but he was not describing hippies. They were Bouzingos, a remarkably similar French youth movement in the 1830s. Dr. Adler added:

At the decline and fall of Rome, during the Renaissance and the Reformation, during the French Revolution and the Napoleonic Wars—in each of these periods we find a social movement and a personality style that emphasizes intuition, immediacy, self-actualization, and transcendence.

He pointed out that drugs have been traditionally used to achieve this state during crisis-riddled times, and that sexual excesses have commonly been noted among youth during periods of intense social change.[1]

Bishop Polycarp in the second century A.D. wrote: "My God, what a wicked century thou hast caused me to live in." Elijah in the ninth century B.C. said: "I, even I only, am left" to worship the one true God.[2]

Dennis the Menace, asking what Thanksgiving was all about, was told by his mother that the Pilgrims had only their homes, food and friends, none of the luxuries we now have, and that we should be grateful. Dennis asked, "No ice cream soda, or TV, or electric trains?"

"No."

"Know what I'm grateful for? That I wasn't a Pilgrim!"

As we look back over the pages of history, it can cause us to be grateful that we live in today's world!

Half the people who have ever lived are alive today! In 1830 there were one billion people on our planet. By 1930 there were two billion, and by 1960 three billion. Today it stands at three and one-half billion. By the year 2000, if the population growth continues at the same rate, there will be seven billion people looking for standing room and something to eat. And yet, man has emerged from worse crises and solved problems equally as threatening.

In the realm of national morality we recall that in the eighteenth century, England fought a war to force the opium trade on China. Lest we forget our own national sins, the treatment accorded the American Indian has been one of the worse blots on our record. At one time they were exterminated as if they were diseased rats, and our treatment of them today does not do us credit.

The "Good Old Days"

When we look back nostalgically to older times, thinking them better than today, we forget what they were really like. In the Middle Ages the light of learning went out in Europe. Only a tiny fraction of the population of Europe during that period could read, and education was available almost exclusively in monasteries. Only in the Arab world was there any progress in the field of education or science. The Arabs had great universities in Cairo, Baghdad and Cordova, where astronomy, medicine, and mathematics flourished.

Witches were believed in by educated persons only a few hundred years ago. Martin Luther said, "I would burn them all." Sir William Harvey, who discovered the circulation of the blood less than two hundred and seventy-five years ago, believed in the power of witches. An estimated forty thousand of them were executed in the seventeenth century alone.

Smallpox swept over Europe unhindered in the sixteenth century, and it was the scourge of our country until fifty or sixty years ago. The Black Plague descended on Europe in the Middle Ages, killing approximately 40 percent of the population. In eighteenth-century England half of all children died before the age of five.

At late as one hundred years ago, operations were horrible affairs, with patients strapped down screaming with pain. Arms and legs were amputated without the use of anesthetics, which had not yet been discovered. No one knew about germs, and surgeons operated under conditions of incredible filth. Most patients died on the operating table.

Sometimes we tend to imagine that in the "good old days" everyone went to church. But in Princeton, in 1792, there was only one professing Christian. In Yale, during the same period, students were largely athletic, often drunk, and openly immoral. Harvard fared little better. In 1838 President Quincy called the faculty together to announce the dynamiting of the chapel by students, as if they hadn't heard the explosion. A plot to dynamite the library was discovered the same day.

Six hundred years ago people were burned at the stake for translating the Bible into English, and thousands were imprisoned for reading the Bible. William Tyndale's efforts to translate the Bible were opposed and suppressed and eventually he was condemned for heresy and executed in 1536. Only three hundred years ago, Bunyan, whose *Pilgrim's Progress* was written in Bedford Jail, was sentenced to twelve years in that dank and dreary prison for the crime of preaching the gospel in the open fields.

In Chicago, one hundred years ago, the First Baptist Church was asked if they would permit the use of their building for a Sunday school. The request was denied, the deacons replying that "it is too worldly a purpose for a church."

In 1790, Wilberforce, the English statesman, declared: "I dare not marry. The future is too dark and uncertain." In 1780, William Pitt declared, "There is scarcely anything around us but ruin and despair." Disraeli moaned in the nineteenth century that "in industry, commerce and agriculture there is no hope." The Duke of Wellington said on his deathbed: "I thank God I am spared the ruin that is gathering about us."

J. C. Penney, founder of the chain of retail stores bearing his name, recalled the time when his father was put on trial before his church for teaching that ministers should be paid, so that they could devote full time to the ministry. The church solemnly voted him out of membership. His wife sprang to her feet in the balcony and shouted, "I believe as he does." They expelled her from membership, too.

This quote from a national periodical has a familiar ring:

It is a gloomy moment in history. Not in the lifetime of most people has there been such grave apprehension. Never has the future seemed so uncertain as this. In France the political cauldron seethes and bubbles with uncertainty. Russia hangs, as usual, like a cloud, dark and silent upon the horizon or Europe. All the resources and energies of the British empire are sorely tried . . . in coping with vast and deadly problems, and there are disturbed conditions in China. Of our own troubles in the United States no man can see the end. Fortunately they are as yet mainly commercial. The very haste to be rich is the occasion of much widespread calamity, and has tended to destroy moral forces.

This appeared in *Harper's Magazine* one hundred years ago.

Between 3000 B.C. and A.D. 1400, there were probably only five really important technological innovations: the general use of iron, paved roads, voting, coinage, and long-distance water supply. We have seen more inventions, improvements and social advancement in the last six months than during that entire span of four thousand four hundred years!

Recently, I counted twenty-six different functions in our home performed by electricity. I was listening to the stereo, eating ice cream from the freezer, with an electric vibrator on my back while doing the counting. My wife said, "No Roman emperor ever had it so good." I replied, "If I ever grumble again, please stop me."

A short two hundred years ago homes were lit by the same kind of candles or oil lamps in use for thousands of years. The techniques of daily living had advanced only slightly over what they had been fifteen hundred years before. People traveled at the same speed and in the same manner as they had for centuries. News traveled no faster two hundred years ago than it did in the time of Nero, or of Abraham for that matter. As late as 1800 there were two hundred crimes punishable by death under English law.

One's chances of living to a "ripe old age" are ten times as great as they were a hundred years ago. Thirty or forty years ago science and religion were quarreling about evolution. Yes, we have made some progress.

Problems Have Always Been with Us

The world will never be without problems. Overpopulation, pollution, the threat of an all-out atomic war, racial injustice, poverty, moral problems and a hundred other issues still remain to be solved. Each generation will face its own particular set of crises; but in order to preserve our sanity and maintain some degree of faith and hope, it is essential that we glance up from the horrors of the daily paper and look back into history to see how far we have come.

Roger Babson, the late economist, once said, "I can, within one hour, banish worry and turn myself into an utter optimist. I enter my library, and walk to the shelves containing only books on history. With my eyes shut I reach for a book, not knowing whether I am picking up Prescott's 'Conquest of Mexico,' or Suetonius' 'Lives of the Twelve Caesars.' With my eyes still closed I open the book at random. I then open my eyes and read for an hour, and the more I read, the more I realize that the world has always been in the throes of agony. History fairly shrieks with tragic tales of war, famine, poverty, pestilence, and man's inhumanity to man. After reading for an hour, I realize that bad as conditions are now, they are infinitely better than they used to be. This enables me to see and face my present troubles in their proper perspective."

In some areas, of course, we have lost ground. Back in the days of the horse and buggy the average speed of vehicles on the streets of New York City was thirteen miles an hour. Today, in the age of high speed, and racing to the moon, the average speed is seven miles an hour on Manhattan's streets!

I read recently a report exposing some atrocious conditions existing in many of our prisons. I was depressed to think that our society could condone such a situation. Then I recalled a recent visit to an amazing California penal institution where twelve hundred young men are "incarcerated." This word hardly applies, for this is an educational institution—a Youth Training School. Through there is a high wire fence surrounding the area, and a few guard towers, everything else about the institution is just about what one would expect in a first-class school. Twenty trades are taught, high school classes are conducted since most of the young men are school dropouts and the general atmosphere is considerably better than I have observed in many public schools.

The officials are humane, compassionate, and highly trained for their jobs. A hundred years ago or less these young men would have been locked in tiny cells, with no opportunity to learn a trade, exercise or mingle freely. Infraction of rules would have resulted in physical punishment sometimes amounting to torture. When those young men return to society, they are not branded as felons. They have skills which they learned in the school, and more self-respect in most instances than they had acquired in the first eighteen years of their lives! Candor compels us to acknowledge that there are prisons today little advanced over penal practices of fifty or one hundred years ago. But slowly, inexorably, man is making progress.

In the last fifty years man has learned more than he had previously learned in all recorded history; in the last ten years he has learned more than he did in the previous fifty years, and in the last five years he has learned more than in the previous ten. Whether this knowledge will be used creatively or destructively is up to us. We are in charge!

Civilization is standing on a long tightrope over a yawning abyss. We have accumulated knowledge necessary to rescue our world from threatened chaos, or to destroy it in a series of atomic blasts. Knowledge we have in abundance. The question remains: do we have the *wisdom* to use this knowledge wisely?

Lest we be plunged into bleak despair and pessimism by the repetitious newscasts which stress man's depravity and mistakes, let us take a somewhat broader view of the situation.

Modern viewers-with-alarm who want to change the system, and who paint the picture very black, could do well to take stock of what the present generation has accomplished:

Signs of Hope

Within the lifetime of many people now living, life expectancy has increased by 50 percent. Ours is a far healthier world than it was thirty or fifty years ago; so much so that this very fact poses a new threat, that of overpopulation. In the same period of time this much-maligned generation has found a way to rid our country of the fear of epidemics of typhus, diphtheria, smallpox, scarlet fever, measles and mumps. The once-dreaded polio and tuberculosis are virtually unheard of. Most adults today lived through the world's worst depression, emerged from World War II, recovered, and helped rebuild a ravaged European continent.

The so-called Establishment, now decried on every hand as reactionary and evil, had a hand in raising the standard of living for more people than ever before in the history of mankind. This generation has made it possible for young people to be the tallest, healthiest, and probably best looking generation of youth ever to inhabit the earth. Along with this, our laws, however imperfect, grant dissident voices the right to protest the inequities which still exist.

This current generation of Americans, decried and condemned as hopeless, has enabled more people to work fewer hours for more money than ever before. The Establishment, with all of its faults, has enabled more people to travel and attend school than any civilization in history. Higher education is now possible for millions of young people who, without having done their homework in history, believe that our generation has failed them.

Faulty though they may be—since human beings are faulty—our efforts to erase racial distinctions and wipe out poverty have produced more results in the past twenty or thirty years than in the previous two hundred.

There have been blunders and mistakes all along the line, as there will always be. The ivory tower idealist and the unkempt anarchist have joined forces. With no other credentials than arrest records for violent protest, bomb-throwing, or a penchant for making fiery speeches, they castigate the Establishment as all bad, and portray themselves as harbingers of the good news of a great new civilization in which there will be nothing but peace, prosperity and love.

They have loved peace so much that they destroyed over three hundred million dollars worth of university property (including some banks, which were supposed to be linked to the evil conspiracy). Only a handful of these have suffered any penalty more severe than a few months in a county jail. Most were not arrested, because our laws permit "honest dissent."

There have been few periods in history when there was neither war, privation, dishonesty, pestilence, or poverty. Man has struggled toward his ideal through the ages at great cost in terms of blood, sorrow, and tears, and from time to time we perceive some advance.

Fortunately we know how the story ends. John in the Revelation unfolds the secret culmination of the ages.

I heard a great voice from the throne saying, "Behold, the dwelling of God is with men. He will dwell with them and they shall be his people, and God himself will be with them; and he will wipe away every tear from their eyes, and death shall be no more, neither shall there be mourning nor crying nor pain any more, for the former things have passed away."[3]

5

Love, Not Legalism

> "A new commandment I give to
> you, that you love one another."[1]
> —Jesus

I WAS in my study the Sunday before Christmas, feeling the slight depression I normally experience around the Christmas season. It usually disappears around the second day of January.

As I left my study and went out into the hall and toward the sanctuary, I met a young couple whom I had been counseling off and on for two or three years. Theirs had been a miserable marriage; we had made little progress. It had reached a point a few weeks before when he said he didn't want any part of her or the marriage, and she had stormed out of the study in a rage.

She came back later, and I gave her a book to read dealing with the woman's part in the marriage. She phoned later and berated me with great hostility for giving her the book. "You and the book and everyone else tell me it's all my fault. I'm sick of the book, and you, and my parents and my husband. I wish I were dead."

"Look," I said gently, "just read a little more, and I'll be praying about the situation. Let's see what happens."

I learned later that as things became even more desperate she had picked up the book and begun to read it again. Then she began to apply some of the principles outlined in the book. Her attitude changed radically, and in response he had begun to melt.

As I met them in the hall that Sunday morning, I was surprised to see them beaming. I paused and put my arms around them.

"How's it going?"

"Wonderful," she said.

"Do you love him?" I asked her.

"Yes," she smiled radiantly.

"Do you love her?"

He smiled, "Yeah! It's great. Things couldn't be better."

I hugged them both, and something happened to me. I felt warm and wonderful. Their new love for each other and for God did something to me. I began to feel a bit of the Christmas spirit.

In the pulpit a little later as I opened up the church bulletin, I saw written on the outside, "We love you, Dr. O. The Cast." I smiled. The Cast was the group which was to present the Christmas pageant that morning. Some youngster wrote that, I thought. How nice.

A few minutes later several members of the cast slipped in through the side door and sat near me, waiting for their entry. One of them leaned over and whispered, "Dr. O, did you get your note?" I blinked. Oh, that note on the church bulletin. "Yes," I whispered. "Great! I love you too." Christmas was moving in on me, and my usual mild depression was vanishing. More important, I was experiencing some of the love which characterized the early church before it became an institution.

During the pageant a couple sang a new and lovely rendition of *The Birthday of a King*. It was beautiful, soaring, triumphant. I began to feel something too deep for words or explanation. My analytical mind tried to sort out the feelings and label them. "Ridiculous," I thought. "Why try to analyze feelings like this?"

During the pageant, which I could see only partially from where I was seated, I caught a glimpse of a young woman as she lifted her face heavenward with a look of such beauty and radiance that I felt uplifted, inspired and thrilled. She was a lovely girl, with an inner beauty and love that reached out to everyone.

Now something powerful was beginning to reach me. It was love and God and wonder and awe and reverence and beauty, all in one great big emotion. I wanted to be alone and give way to the feeling, and let loose the flood of tears which were back there someplace—but one doesn't do that in our culture. Too bad. The choir ended with the "Hallelujah Chorus," and that did it! Beyond words and logic or thought I was feeling what I imagined the early Christians felt in their love feasts.

After the service two lovely little girls who always sat in the balcony with their mother came by and lifted their faces for a kiss. This Sunday ritual had been going on for a couple of years. That particular morning I saw them as more radiantly beautiful than I had ever perceived them before. They were pure and beautiful manifestations of God, giving and receiving love.

Then the stream of worshippers began emerging. I said the conventional things, shook hands with them, but for some reason I wanted to hug each of them. We were all one in the love of Christ, one in some mystical sense we cannot fully perceive, but can feel.

This, I thought, is what Christianity is all about—love, not creeds and dogmas, important as they are. The church was meant to be the Body of Christ, a gathering of individuals who can all merge into one through love for Christ.

I am not saying that one can go through life in a constant state of euphoria (though that would be nice!). There are the manifold duties and irritations of life. Tempers flare, misunderstandings arise. Any movement needs some form and structure, and so organizations are born; and then we spend most of our time and energy promoting the organization.

We are in charge—you and I— of our spiritual lives. No one else can assume responsibility for us at this point. We can settle for a mundane, routine, religious life, a legalistic set of religious dos and don'ts, or we can seek out a Christian fellowship which offers us an opportunity to tune in on the wavelength of love, the hallmark of the early church.

I have found some of this radiant, contagious love in a Roman Catholic Church in Oakland, California. My wife said to the priest as we left a thrilling, warm service where love engulfed everyone, "I am a Baptist minister's wife, but I'd join your church if I lived on this side of the Bay." He replied, "We'd welcome you!"

I've experienced that same quality of loving fellowship in

a Southern Baptist church with a membership so vast that I could not see how they maintained the atmosphere of warmth; yet it was there. I experienced it again in an Episcopal church in New England, and was at a loss to account for it until I discovered that more than half the church members were members of Yokefellow groups.

Someone has pointed out that the church at times seems to be a nagging wife instead of the loving bride of Christ, a tradition-encrusted hierarchy whose energies are devoted more to survival than renewal. The liberal, social action-oriented church too often has little to offer beyond a program for improved race relations, peace drives, and ecological crusades. Good as these things are—and they are good—it does little or nothing for the lonely, the bereaved, the warring family, or the individual alienated from himself, from God and from his neighbor.

At the other end of the theological spectrum, there are the extremely conservative churches, with their deadly legalism and moralistic approach to life. They provide the terribly insecure individual with the security of a dogmatic set of beliefs and religious clichés.

In the middle, reaching out in either direction from time to time, are the bulk of the churches, not always certain just where to place the emphasis. Their dilemma is in not knowing how much of their energy to expend excoriating evildoers, promoting good works in the community, visiting the sick and lonely, encouraging open housing, or supporting the local drug abuse crusade. The minister is often caught between the current "in thing" being promoted that year by his denomination, the needs of individuals in his congregation, and the demands placed upon him by the community.

The church is not the edifice on the corner, nor a set of denominational officials. It is *us*. We are in charge. We need not assume responsibility for changing the structure of the church, but we are each responsible for our spiritual lives. We are in charge of that! And God seeks first to help each of us toward wholeness, then to work through us as channels through which he can bring others to wholeness.

Jennie was a completely compliant child. She buried all of her resentment over the failure of either parent to express any genuine love. When she was about eighteen, she walked out. She ended up in New York City. Recounting the sordid details of the next few years would serve no purpose. The buried rebellion emerged in an astounding variety of forms, all dangerous and antisocial.

Later, abandoned by a brilliant but totally amoral husband, she and her child found themselves on their own.

Jennie had a good mind, some significant talents, and an enormous inferiority complex. She had always felt unloved and unlovely. She had difficulty in believing anyone could really love her. But in a nearby church she found total acceptance and friends. On one level of her personality she was in open rebellion against God and Christian people. At another level she was seeking God and love. Then in a Yokefellow group she began the experiment of trying to let people love her. The fear of opening up and risking possible rejection battled against the deeper need to belong.

It may take years for the scars of childhood to heal; but she is accepting the responsibility for her own life. She is in charge, and knows it. She is part of a church, and part of a fellowship group, through which she is seeking the wholeness that comes only from God. She senses that God works through people, and that as she can let them in, and trust them, God's love is being mediated to her through them.

Will the New Testament Church Be Revived?

For over twelve years I met with a group of ministers every Friday morning. We called it a Yokefellow group, and spent an hour and a half or more each week sharing at a feeling level. At one point a young minister and a leading layman from his church began to participate. The layman was a young physician, and the first nonclergyman who had ever been invited to meet with us. He seemed to qualify by virtue of his deep devotion to his church, and because his father was a minister. He spoke our language. Our concerns were his.

For nearly a year the young physician and his minister struggled with the problem of belonging to a rigid, tradition-bound church geared more to the nineteenth than to the twentieth century. Loving the church, they hated to leave it; yet they could not endure the stern, moralistic approach of their denomination.

In nearly every group session they shared their concern and ambivalence, but eventually they resolved their conflict. They and about twenty like-minded members elected to establish a "home church." There was sufficient financial backing to pay the minister. At first there was no desire to break ties with their denomination, but their joyous, loving, tradition-shattering meetings on Sunday and during the week were so threatening to denominational leaders that a break eventually took place.

Services in the new young church are not formal. The observance of the Lord's Supper is a celebration instead of a solemn ritual. Sharing, fellowship, and joy have replaced the legalistic trappings of their old church.

The physician discovered among his patients many whose physical ailments were obviously related to spiritual and emotional problems. A score or more of these were invited to meet with him and their minister, and several Yokefellow groups were formed. At the outset the members were asked to take one of the spiritual growth inventories provided by Yokefellows, Inc., the West Coast branch of the Yokefellow movement.

The inventory consists of a standardized psychological test with a weekly or bi-weekly feedback system of evaluation slips. These are sent to the leader, who passes them out to the members, who may read them in the group if they wish. The evaluation slip pinpoints some area of the personality in need of growth. The experience is neither embarrassing nor threatening in any way, since all are receiving similar slips. The chief value of the process is not the psychological test, but the weekly slips which result from the test. These have a carefully balanced emphasis upon the spiritual and the psychological nature of man. More than sixty thousand individuals have taken these spiritual growth inventories since they were first introduced in this form some years ago.

The "home church" outgrew a home and soon began meeting in a pizza parlor, later moving to their own building. Virtually all of the members belong to Yokefellow groups. They not only become acquainted; they come to know each other at a deep level, and out of this grows a deep love for each other. It is a church based on love and fellowship, rather than doctrine. They feel that "if the Son makes you free, you will be free indeed."[2] Their freedom is a sense of being liberated from tradition and creedal statements. Their loyalty is not to a denominational hierarchy, but to Christ.

In saying this I do not disparage denominations, or the need for form and structure; but when Christians lose sight of their goal, and redouble their efforts, little can result but organized allegiance to creeds and programs.

A Loving Fellowship Vs. a Legalistic System

The Christian church began as a loving fellowship. Until A.D. 325 there were no church buildings, since Christianity was an illicit religion. Little groups of people met in homes. "The church in thy house"[3] is a reference to the "home church"—presumably the common form. It was in those first three hundred years that the Christian church had its period of greatest growth.

When Christianity was legalized, it became possible for the church to own property; so the Christians came out of their "home churches," had a building-fund drive, and proceeded to promote large congregations. In the process they lost intimacy and fellowship. The church was no longer a loving fellowship but an organization. It is impossible to love a hundred or a thousand other members for the simple reason that one cannot know that many people at a deep level.

Love and mutual concern was the cohesive force of the church until A.D. 325, when it became an institution. Now a new "glue" was needed to hold it together. This was found in doctrines. The fellowship of love became a fellowship of people who believed certain doctrines. Those who believed a particular set of doctrines became one denomination. Those who held different doctrinal views formed another. This eventually culminated in the unbelievable spectacle of Christians burning "heretics" at the stake because they were not "orthodox."

The next step downward came when the church, still holding onto creeds for dear life, became moralistic. "Doctrinally right and morally pure" became the spoken or unspoken goal. There is obviously nothing wrong with believing the "right" things and being morally pure; but a problem arises when we try to determine what the "correct" doctrines really are, and then to agree on what constitutes morality. By some strange quirk of human nature the word "moral" became almost universally equated with sexual morality, which reveals something interesting about ourselves!

A single lapse into sexual immorality could result in expulsion from the church membership, whereas one could indulge in character assassination, gossip, lust, materialism, greed, and avarice, and remain a leading light in the congregation. Some of the meanest people I have ever known have believed all of the "right" things; and I have known hostile, unloving, unforgiving people who violated every spiritual concept given by Jesus, who managed to remain in good standing in a church. Hawthorne's *Scarlet Letter* points up the evil of permitting Christianity to become creedal, moralistic, and unloving.

There are some fundamental moral laws in the universe, but Jesus did not intend his church to be based upon either a set of doctrines or upon legalistic, moralistic concepts.

Jesus tried to help man solve the threefold problem: alienation from self, from God, and from others. Love is the only force that can enable us to accomplish this. Jesus put it simply and succinctly when he stated that one can fulfill the entire law by loving God with all of one's nature, and loving one's neighbor as he loves himself. And to love oneself properly is tremendously important, for unless we can love ourselves we are incapable of loving others.

The Apostle Paul stated in his letter to the Christians of Galatia, "The fruit of the Spirit is love, joy, peace, patience, kindness, goodness, faithfulness gentleness self-control."[4] Most people I know would settle for one or two of these nine dividends—particularly the first three: love, joy, and peace. These fruits are a far cry from the rather joyless exercises indulged in during a typical Sunday morning worship service.

Elsewhere, Paul says, "For the kingdom of God does not mean food and drink but righteousness and peace and *joy* in the Holy Spirit."[5] The very night in which he was betrayed, the night before his crucifixion, Jesus told the twelve disciples, "These things I have spoken to you, that my *joy* may be in you, and that your *joy* may be full."[6] A bit later he said, "Ask and you will receive, that your *joy* may be full."[7] And Luke related that "the disciples were filled with *joy* and with the Holy Spirit."[8] Most churches and many Christians today know little about joy or love.

Channels of God's Love

One Sunday morning a man dropped in to see me before the service. How I dreaded those unexpected, unannounced visitors who came in to sit and visit for fifteen or twenty minutes just before the morning service! This man had bored me for years with tales of himself and his early life. His one subject was himself. He used no periods, or semicolons; just commas. There was no shutting him off. He never made appointments, and always came at the most inopportune time.

My visitor was not a member of the church, but I had known him for more than thirty years. I had suffered much at his hands. Now he came barging in, talking a steady stream of minutiae.

I sighed wearily as he entered my study without knocking, but a compulsive talker is never aware of the feelings of others. I knew he would stay for half an hour talking trivia, all dealing with himself, his exploits, his comings and goings. I listened with mounting irritation. "Love, joy, peace . . ." I felt none of these; just gross exasperation. At five minutes to eleven I rose to leave.

He said, "Could we pray together?" I said, "You lead us, won't you?" I bit my lip after I said it, for I suddenly realized we would be in for an interminable prayer.

He came close and we stood there while he prayed. I ceased to listen, and put my arm around him, saying to myself, "This man has an insatiable need for love, as all compulsive talkers do. Maybe I can give him a little." As I drew him closer with my arm around his shoulder, I remembered some of the details of his early life of deprivation and utter poverty. He had never known his own parents, and had had virtually no formal education. Yet, I recalled, he had achieved significantly in a field where an education is normally an absolute requisite. I reached back into his childhood and found a lonely child feeling abandoned by parents, and only half-wanted by his foster parents. I began to feel some of his childhood anguish and rejection.

He prayed on and on, and suddenly it was all right, because in imagination I was reaching out to take the hand of that lonely child. I carried on an imaginary conversation with him, and felt some of his pain.

I don't know how long the prayer lasted. It didn't matter any more. I drew closer, hugged him, and loved him— loved the lonely little boy who grew up to be a man still begging to be loved. He will go to his grave asking to be noticed, to be loved, to be cared about. And, I asked myself, what are we here for but to love one another?

I had no love to give. No one has. Any love we express is God's love channeled through us. "The Father that dwelleth in me, he doeth the works," Jesus said.[9] Even Jesus had no love within himself, except as he was a channel of God's infinite love. And because he was a pure, unselfish channel, he could express it as no one else has, before or since.

True Christianity is love—not morality, or good deeds, or social justice. These all flow out of love, or they will be tinged with neurotic egocentricity. This love may be expressed by one person in terms of trying to bring social justice into the world. Another will minister to the sick, and still another may carry a banner protesting some social injustice. Some will preach it, some simply live it, others act it out in manifold ways. But believe me, love is the name of the game—the essence of Christianity.

Some time ago I met a black ex-convict who had been released from prison after serving a thirty-year term. Something had happened to him in prison; and when he came out the first thing he did was to find a job. Almost immediately thereafter he got a few people together and rented an old house in the center of the worst slum area he could find. A sign on the outside read, "Channel of Love House."

It is neither a church, nor a community center, nor a social service institution, yet it is a little of each of those things. It is basically a place for fellowship. People go there for help, to visit, to worship. My friend and his helpers stand ready to try to meet any need. He is self-effacing and very gentle. He radiates a quiet assurance that he is doing what Christ would have him do. He has no doubts. As he told me of his venture, I had the feeling that it was not just another organization established to help people, but precisely what the name implied: a channel of love. As every institution is but the elongated shadow of a person, his venture is simply an extension of himself. He felt a need to become a channel of divine love. He is not concerned that it be the biggest, or best financed, or the best known. There is no egocentric drive to be famous, just a quiet desire to be a channel through which God's love can manifest itself. "This," I thought, "is what it's all about."

A friend of mine, the minister of a thriving church, told me of a young man who dropped in to ask for help in finding a job. The pastor asked, "What kind of work do you do?" The young man said with quiet earnestness, "My work is to do the will of God."

My friend said, "I sensed that I was talking either to a nut or to a very rare kind of person." Further discussion revealed that the young man was genuine. His primary purpose in life was to do the will of God. Earning a living was secondary; it was only the means by which he supported himself while he sought to know and do the will of God.

This sort of attitude is suspect in our religious framework. We like to read about St. Francis of Assisi, who would not be classed as one of the best balanced personalities of all time, though surely one of the most remarkable. But when we come face to face with such an individual we scarcely know what to do with him. He doesn't "fit" into any of our standard slots.

Spiritual Breakthroughs and the Established Church

Today some of the most exciting discoveries in the realm of the spirit are being made by other than recognized religious leaders. A lengthy article in a national magazine states that "the saints of organized religion have lost influence in recent years, but the kind of religious experience usually associated with saints is being discovered in the laboratory." A husband-wife team of experimental psychologists in New York City has concluded, on the basis of extensive experiments with normal, healthy persons, that "the brain-mind system has a contact point with what is experienced as God, fundamental reality, or the profoundly sacred."[10]

Using a variety of non-drug stimuli such as meditation, sound and light environments to induce altered states of consciousness, the experimenters enabled a reporter to experience a journey into the center of her being.

> I felt so ecstatically the sensation of flight [she reported]—free, joyous, yet peaceful, ever deeper to the center of my being, until I was conscious of an indescribable unity within myself and with all things. Finally I felt as if I had flown to the core of life itself.

She had always been deeply disturbed by the injustices of life, and sought to find an answer to this age-old problem:

> I had vivid mental images of real-life horrors throughout history, like the Inquisition and the Holocaust of the Jews during World War II. I saw the petty injustices that people commit against each other every day . . . I saw the poor strangling in the disease and dirty ugliness of the slums. It became clear to me that no amount of legislation or education will ever dispel completely the force of ingrained racial prejudice and that no degree of virtue among the enlightened will extinguish the evil that breeds wars.
>
> I became more and more sorrowful at what I envisaged (indeed tears were streaming down my face); yet increasingly I could "see" in the most profound way I have ever known that the beauty of life far exceeds the sorrow, the injustice.
>
> . . I was aware of my unity with all the people who have ever suffered, from the victims of petty lies to those killed by untold wars, persecutions and centuries of mistrust and hate. But paradoxically I understood quite vividly that life triumphs over all this misery even though it cannot erase it. Life is indeed "stronger than death"—not just in the religious sense, but quite literally. . . . I was aware of smiling and crying at once. An immense resignation and peace flooded my entire being.

Later she experienced psychological "death" and "rebirth."

> I knew with incredible clarity that life is eternal, despite death. I was overcome with joy at (experiencing) this truth and I wanted to run out on the street and shout it to the New Yorkers plodding homeward from their dull

downtown offices, unaware that a sea of beauty, life and love surrounded and sustained them.

Dr. Robert E. L. Masters and Dr. Jean Houston, who guided her through the experience, said, "Religious institutions are now disintegrating because religion has cut itself off from its principal sources of nourishment—the soul, the symbolic, and mythogenic process, the psychogenic resources." They feel that it is ironic that, in the past decade, mystical experience has again become a beneficent, transforming reality for great numbers of people—but it has been happening outside the major religious institutions.

Many churches and religious leaders, Dr. Masters believes, are deeply suspicious of mystical experience, partly because they associate it with magic, and the occult. He believes, however, that this attitude seriously impairs the survival of institutionalized religion: "The clergyman who dismisses all of this as primitive and regressive is lacking in vision. He had not understood that profound mystical experience can open energy sources to sustain a contemporary religion, and that the clergyman himself should be the guide for this spiritual journey."

John Wesley's followers would have understood what Dr. Masters was talking about, as would the early Quakers. William Sargant, an English psychiatrist, says in *Battle for the Mind* that intellectual indoctrination without emotional excitement is remarkably ineffective, as the empty pews of most English churches prove.

As a minister I find myself in the strange position of feeling defensive when the church and religious values are attacked, but inwardly dissatisfied with the typical business-as-usual, Sunday-morning-at-11:00, highly organized and emotionally unsatisfying worship services conducted in most churches. I feel nostalgic and protective toward the church, and impatient at the same time. I want something to happen—something dynamic, challenging, soul-stirring. Yet, as a pastor I presided over much the same kind of services which I am describing. There is no one to blame; but there is a vast area wide open for exploration: the human mind and spirit. Hosts of men and women—and youth especially—are yearning for someone to show the way. Thank God there are open-minded explorers searching for ways by which the power of God can be released into human life.

Are There Many Paths to God?

I am not prepared to disparage Yoga, which must have something to recommend it; or astrology, which has been kicking around for several thousand years and is now enjoying a revival of interest, though so far no modern scientist has found an iota of evidence to support it. The latest imported Marahashi with his string of devotees probably won't do any serious damage, and may prove of help to some here and there. Each seeker must find his own way. Only the intolerant and bigoted today claim that theirs is the one true faith, that their church is the custodian of all revealed truth.

I am sympathetic with the ecstatic, hand-clapping, orgiastic members of the highly charged, emotional groups who find God in their own way; and I feel a kinship with the liturgical denominations for whom form and ceremony have deep significance. I doubt if God is interested one way or the other *how* we find and relate to him. The important thing is to establish a satisfying, working relationship with the Eternal.

I preached in an Episcopal church in the East one Sunday morning, and they invited me to attend their evening "service." I entered the parish hall with the rector. He was, like everyone else, attired very casually. Most of the men wore no coats. The room was filled with people ranging in age from three to about fifty.

Everyone was sitting on the floor on little pieces of carpet. Five guitars began to play, and everyone joined in singing some informal but beautiful modern songs. A woman read a brief bit of simple liturgy and we sang some more. Then the mood changed and even the youngest children were surprisingly quiet. We were told to choose some person near us and either draw on the blackboard, or make out of materials provided, something to illustrate a significant event of the past week. For fifteen or twenty minutes the pairs worked at their project, and finally returned to their little squares of carpet.

The rector was somewhere across the room. The affair

was entirely in the hands of the members of the congregation. When communion was served, I waited for the minister to participate; but the same woman was presiding. She read some appropriate Scripture, the people responded, and then the baskets of bread were passed. Each person said quietly, as he passed it, "The body of Christ." Three-year-olds, teenagers and adults all participated with the same reverence.

Then the cup was passed from hand to hand after we had read responsively. People were scattered and my orderly mind wondered how they would accomplish this. It was no problem. "The blood of Christ," said the girl to my left, as she passed the cup to me.

Then we sang together, quietly, but with fervor. And suddenly I discovered that I had never been in a communion service quite as meaningful. In fact I was deeply stirred, and I couldn't account for it. There was no organ to stir the senses, no planned solemnity, no choir, no stained glass windows. What was it, I asked myself, that made me feel at one with these people? Why was I so deeply moved? I wanted to go outside and be alone.

Suddenly I knew what it was. It was love! Nearly all of the adults involved were members of Yokefellow groups. In their small groups, and now in this warm, loving fellowship, they had learned to love one another. "A new commandment I give to you, that you love one another,"[11] flashed into my mind. It was love that permeated the entire room, an indescribable sense of oneness and unity and involvement with one another.

I told the minister as he drove me to my motel that I had found it a beautiful experience, and that I could account for it only on the basis of love. He smiled, and said, "The people around town who disapprove of all that informality call it 'Albert's Love-in.'"

"My friend," I told him, "you have a formal morning worship service for those who desire it. There are people who will never want or need anything more than that. Some may never accept anything more than your dignified worship service. But I loved your evening fellowship hour, with communion; and those who are anxious to learn how to love will find their way to it."

After the morning service in that Episcopal church, during the coffee hour, a woman had come over and said rather timidly, "I see all these people touching each other, and hugging one another. They are the ones who have been in groups. I am not a toucher. It bothers me."

I said, "Are you willing to let them express their love that way?"

"Yes, I suppose so." She sounded wistful.

"Is there some part of you that secretly envies them?"

"Yes. But I'm afraid and self-conscious."

Her husband joined us just then and took part in the discussion. He felt much the same as his wife, but he, too, seemed wistful as he saw warm-hearted people embracing one another.

"Do you have to touch people if you join one of these groups?" she asked.

"No," I said. "But I expect that most of these people expressing love have been or are now in groups where they learn to love each other." I took hold of her hand and his. I drew them close and said, "It isn't important how we express the love of which Christ spoke, but most of us, unless we were deprived of love in childhood, feel a need to be touched." I drew them both closer and put my arms around them.

"I sense that as a child you experienced very little demonstration of affection."

"That's right," the man said. "My parents were not demonstrative."

"I don't think you would have brought up the subject if you had not longed to be part of a loving group. Would you like to try it for a month or two? Learning to touch people is not the primary goal; but learning to love God, people, and ourselves, is one dividend of such a group, and then people find many ways of expressing that love."

Just then we were joined by a warm, friendly couple. They entered the conversation, and drew the three of us into a circle of love. With my arm around the husband and wife, I said, "Wouldn't you like to join one of those groups and learn to feel the love you see demonstrated?"

"Yes," the woman said, "it feels good. I'd like to try it."

Her husband smiled and nodded. "We sure need something. Maybe this is what we've been searching for."

God's love is mediated through persons. Perhaps some have experienced it in other ways, but generally I feel confident that divine love becomes personal only through persons.

A friend of mine who had become enormously successful in business, told me something of his life story, after some gentle prodding.

I had detected a kind of all-pervasive sadness in his entire personality. He was friendly, but there was a wistful sadness in his voice. I understood why when he told me about his childhood.

His mother had died when he was quite young. He was reared by his alcoholic father. As a small child he had to cook most of the meals, because his father was usually too drunk to help. "So," he said, "I learned to cook out of sheer necessity. Then, when I was just a kid, I opened a hamburger stand. It prospered and I opened another. Then the hamburger stand became a restaurant, and finally a whole chain of restaurants.

"But," he said, "though I have prospered beyond my wildest dreams, I still do not know how to love. I love my wife as much as I am able to love anyone, but I seem incapable of feeling much love."

They belonged to the country club set, drank pretty heavily, and had no interest whatever in religion. Wanting to adopt a child, they felt it might improve their chances if they belonged to a church. Accordingly, for all the wrong reasons, they united with a nearby church. He was asked to usher, then invited to participate in other areas of the church life. Finally both he and his wife were experiencing something new—fellowship, acceptance, and a new meaning in life.

They realized how phony they had been in uniting with the church initially, but now they no longer felt guilty over that. They began to absorb the spirit of Christ's teachings, and to put these principles to work in their lives.

Doing the right thing for the wrong reason had brought a wonderful new dimension into their lives. In the course of time the husband began to experience a new capacity to give and receive love. More than anything else he sought the will of God in his life. He became involved in any number of worthwhile causes. Both came alive spiritually. They had discovered a new dimension of life, the third level, where one loves God for himself alone. It all came about because they had exposed themselves to the love of God, mediated through persons.

I was conducting a retreat in Washington, D.C. One of the women present told me that she had come to know a prostitute who was looking for help, and had finally gathered up a half dozen more who were willing to meet with her.

She had invited them to meet with her regularly in one of the church parlors. They refused. "We're not church people. We're not their kind . . . I don't think we'd be welcome," one of them said. They all felt unworthy to meet in the church, yet they wanted help. As it turned out there were some objections to her plan from a few church leaders.

I said, "Get in touch with them. Have them meet us in any place of their choice."

The next evening she had them assembled in a tiny office. They looked suspicious and mildly hostile when I was introduced as a minister. Those poor derelicts were frightened, battered children of the Eternal. They didn't feel worthy of entering a church, or of taking up my time.

I said, "Look, girls, I'm not in the least interested in your past. Whatever your weaknesses or blunders may have been, I am absolutely confident that they are no worse than my own mistakes and failures. God loves you as much as anyone else on earth. Jesus loved prostitutes, and one of the reasons for his being rejected was that he fraternized with prostitutes, and people whom the Pharisees called sinners." We talked for an hour or more. They gradually opened up, and agreed to meet weekly with the woman who had befriended them. I complimented her upon her love and compassion. She is a genuine channel of God's love. The Church is ministering through her to those whom Jesus came to save.

It makes no difference *what* you believe, if what you believe makes no difference in your life. Even *believing* in love is not the answer. I do not have a pat formula for learning to love, for each arrives there, it seems, by a different route. But one thing is sure: we must learn to love another, or we shall all perish.

6.

Prayer Isn't What You Say

> "In prosperity men ask too little
> of God. In adversity, too much."
> —IVAN PANIN

I HAD heard for years about the giant trout in Mirror
Lake. A hardy friend of mine had brought back a two-
pounder, but he reported that the lake was almost inacces-
sible.

Camping with a friend on nearby Emerald Lake one
summer, I made a suggestion which, when I reflect upon it,
makes me wonder if the altitude had affected my sanity. I
hate heights, am a poor climber, and dislike hiking. But my
love of fly fishing overcame those handicaps, and I proposed that we try to reach Mirror Lake. My friend pointed
out that there was no trail, and that everyone else who had
made the climb had had a local guide with them.

We set out early the next morning, determined to find
the lake. The first hour or two were not too difficult, but
gradually the slope became more nearly vertical. I had not
looked back and down because heights bother me. Finally I
found myself standing on a narrow rock ledge, and we both
realized at the same instant that we had come to a dead
end. There was no way up. We faced a perpendicular rock
wall. For the first time I looked over my shoulder, and
sheer panic set in when I looked down to the floor of the
little valley. I would hit once or twice on the way down if I

lost my hold, and then there was almost a sheer drop to the valley below. After the initial panic came the terrible realization that an inexperienced climber can climb *up* to places from which he cannot get down. More panic. Then self-condemnation: "How in the world did I ever let myself get into this predicament? What brand of insanity brought me to this?"

While I clung there partially paralyzed with fear, my friend discovered that by inching his way along the ledge to the right he could reach an outcropping above him. In a few minutes he had reached the top. I tried to follow him, but there was no way I could reach the spot on the ledge where he had been standing.

Now he was directly above me, looking down from less than three feet above my head. I said, "Bill, I'm stuck. I don't see any way to get up there, and I can't climb back down." He sat pondering for a moment, looking serious.

Finally Bill took off his belt, looped it, and let it dangle down to where I could reach it. I looked at it and shuddered. It wouldn't have supported fifty pounds, and I had a bitter thought about people who bought cheap belts. I was expending no physical energy except to hold on to an outcropping of rock, but suddenly I was very weak. I wondered about the superhuman strength that fear is supposed to release when the adrenal cortex goes to work in a crisis. I was just barely able to hold on, getting weaker instead of stronger. So, I prayed—a very short prayer: "Lord, if you have anything else for me to do in this world, you'll have to lend a hand."

At that point Bill leaned down and said with unaccustomed confidence, "Take hold of my hand." I did. It was sweaty just like mine. But for some reason I *knew* he could lift me with one arm. And he did. A few seconds later I was lying flat on the cool grass above, breathing a prayer of deep gratitude.

Bill said, "I suddenly knew that I could lift you. I was stronger than I have ever been before in my life. I could have pulled up two people at that instant."

Beautiful Mirror Lake was just yards away, sparkling in the afternoon sun. Before we began fishing we explored other possible ways of getting back down. From that vantage point we could see that there was a much longer but safer route back to the valley. It involved clambering over huge boulders, but it was much less dangerous than our ascent.

A crisis brings all of our spiritual and mental resources into sharp focus, but faith is never born in a crisis. One who awaits disaster before learning the meaning of prayer is in for a shock.

Prayer at its highest and best is simply communion with God. If I never thought about God, or communed with him, or expressed gratitude to him, I would feel pretty sheepish about calling on him in a crisis.

Trying to Manipulate God

For ten years or more I enjoyed the friendship of a fellow-minister living in another city. He was brilliant, highly successful, and a very delightful person. One Saturday night when I was deeply engrossed in studying he phoned from the airport. He had two hours between planes and wanted to see me. I explained that I was quite busy, but he insisted that it was very important. Rather reluctantly I went to the airport and met him. It turned out that he wanted something—a very special favor. I said I would see what I could do.

On the way home it hit me with full force. I could recall half a dozen times my friend had phoned or written or come to see me about something he wanted. Then I realized that without exception whenever he had initiated a meeting, it was because he had wanted something from me. He was a manipulator, had always been a manipulator. I recalled other friends who had used that term in describing him, but I had ignored it, for I had genuinely liked him. Yet they were right, and suddenly the friendship vanished. It was as if a door had been slammed shut by the realization of having been used over and over.

I am sure that God has more patience than mortals, but I doubt if he appreciates being "used" and manipulated any more than we do. He wants our fellowship, not simply our frantic calls for help when we are desperate.

The Possibilities of Prayer

There are many facets to prayer: adoration, supplication, praise, communion—and many others. Perhaps one could not, in a lifetime, exhaust all the possibilities inherent in prayer. It is safe to say that few avail themselves of all the benefits potentially available through the channel of prayer.

Sir Arthur Eddington, one of the greatest English scientists of the twentieth century, once said, "I believe that the mind has the power to affect groups of atoms, and even alter atomic behavior; that even the course of the world is not determined by physical laws, but may be altered . . . by thoughts of human beings."

Dr. Walter Dill Scott, physicist and former president of Northwestern University, once said, "Success or failure . . . is caused more by mental attitudes than by mental capabilities."

When someone asked Jesus for healing, he said, "According to your faith be it done to you."[1] He was saying, in essence, that it is not up to God, who wills our best. It all hinges upon our *belief*, our mental attitude, the extent of our faith.

I was visiting a woman who had suffered a serious heart attack. A devout Christian, she was unafraid of death, and smiled as she handed me an envelope. "That contains instructions for my funeral," she said. I put it in my pocket. I knew that she expected me to pray with her, or for her, but for some reason I delayed, looking around the room. An oxygen tank stood beside her bed. Her Bible lay on a table within reach. I held her hand and suggested that instead of talking to God we sit in silence and visualize things the way God wanted them. Finally I said, "I don't feel any need to pray verbally. We are in prayer when we are communicating with him silently. In my mind I just saw you entering the church. I saw you well and strong, able to get around and live a normal life."

"You did? You saw that?"

"Yes. I wasn't trying to see anything. It simply floated onto my mental screen."

"I believe you," she said.

Hers was not an instantaneous healing, but some weeks later she walked into church alone and unaided. Later she took a trip to Hawaii. Fifteen years after that she phoned to ask if I would send back her funeral plans as she wanted to revise them.

At Lystra the Apostle Paul saw a man crippled from

birth, "who had never walked in his life. . . . Paul . . . saw that he had the faith to be cured, so he said to him in a loud voice, 'Stand up straight on your feet'; and he sprang up and started to walk.'" It was not any power in Paul which wrought the healing. He had the capacity to perceive latent faith, and linked that human faith with the divine, beneficent energy always available to those who believe.

In the case of the woman with the heart attack, there was no supplication, no earnest invoking of the healing power of Christ. But the woman's capacity for faith made it possible for me to "see" as a reality that she could live.

It is only infrequently that I am in the emotional and spiritual state which makes this possible. Invariably it is when I am relaxed, at peace within myself, and am unhurried. "Haste delays the things of God," as Meister Eckhart put it.

One's emotional condition has much to do with the degree to which prayer is effective. Whether we call it an emotional, spiritual, or mental attitude is not important. Essentially it is when one's whole being is "in tune" that prayer seems most effective. A negative or doubting attitude is self-defeating, whether in prayer or in any other aspect of life.

Self-Fulfilling Prophecies and Prayer

There are such things as self-fulfilling prophecies. If one makes a firm resolution, involving mental and emotional states, and holds onto this at a deep level, consciously or unconsciously, some kind of results invariably follow.

Fifty years after I made a resolution, I saw with amazement that it had been a self-fulfilling prophecy. I was in grade school when my two older sisters graduated from high school. Both gave graduation addresses. I had a slight speech impediment, and was dreadfully shy. I recall sitting there listening to my sisters, and saying to myself, "If you have to make a speech when you graduate, *I will never graduate.*"

And I didn't! I finished high school, but managed to find a logical way (without being consciously aware of the real reason) to be out of the city on graduation night.

I rebelled at taking required courses in college, and rationalized that it was because I had no use for science, higher mathematics, and languages (which was true enough). So I simply went to college for five years, took the courses I wanted, and quit. I had all of the credits I needed, but did not "graduate." In seminary I gave in and took the courses required for graduation, and got a diploma, but it just "happened" that I had already left for my first church before graduation. I was vaguely aware that I had no interest in graduation ceremonies, but it did not occur to me that I was acting out a self-fulfilling prophecy when I told a seminary official to mail my diploma to me. He said that rules forbade it. I replied as I walked out of his office, "Then just forget it. It's not that important."

"Well, we'll make an exception," he said.

I didn't even look at it when it arrived. I had fulfilled my firm, prophetic resolution. I never "graduated."

Mental attitudes determine destiny, even when they are unconscious. Whether we term it faith, belief, mental attitudes, mind set, or something else, we end up very much with what we expect. It is according to our faith (belief) that it is done to us.

The Power of Belief—Negative and Positive

Belief, whether negative or positive, is powerful. A little girl of five or six asked her father to teach her to sing. But when he tried to teach her to sing the scales, she blundered a few times. In exasperation he said as he pushed her away, "This child will never learn to sing." And she didn't. She was a woman in her forties when she related the incident. As she discusses it she said, "I can't even carry a tune, and I get a sick feeling in my stomach every time I think about that childhood experience."

A similar incident occurred with a boy of seven, except that it was a schoolteacher in his case who instilled the negative thought. I knew him as a young man in his twenties, wondering why he was the only person in the congregation who stood mute while everyone else was singing. He discussed it with me, and announced that he knew he was tone deaf. I said I doubted it very much. I asked him to have a few sessions with our choir director. In a very short time he could sing as well as the next person, and eventually led the singing for young people, and at the family night dinners. However, he reported, "I am always wringing wet with perspiration when I finish." The input had been very strong, and he was still fighting against it.

In both instances the child had believed what the adult had said. What else *would* a child believe? A mental block was formed in this manner. In childhood we learn that some things are possible, and that other things are impossible. These beliefs become part of the basic assumptions upon which we run our lives. A positive input can become as helpful as a negative one can be deadly and self-defeating.

An atheist and a Christian got into an argument about the existence of God. After an hour or so of futile debate, the atheist said in considerable exasperation, "When I talk to an obstinate, irrational person like you, *I thank God* I am as atheist." Intellectually he did not believe in the existence of God, but at a feeling level there was still a strong residue of some childhood teachings which carried over into adulthood.

Louise had received very little love as a child. Several marriages ended in disaster. When I first became acquainted with her, she was undergoing a series of operations. In the next few years she was operated on at least a dozen times. Word would be received that Louise was in the hospital, and her friends would rush there to visit her. No matter how serious the operation (and most of them were major) she was always sitting up in bed, glowing radiantly, her hair done professionally and her makeup on. She usually looked happier than the people visiting her.

But after leaving the hospital she would begin to look woebegone. The details of her pain, the number of hours on the operating table, the symptoms, all provided her with conversational matter for some months at the most. Soon she would begin to suffer from other symptoms, always in a different part of her anatomy. Back in the hospital there was always a repetition of the scenario. The radiant, smiling Louise would greet her sympathetic friends, getting from them *the only kind of love she knew how to accept*. There is no condemnation in my recital of her problem, for it was very real. Th only way she had ever discovered to get love was by being carved up. She had never experienced genuine love, and had to settle for pity. I am confident that her "mind set" was nothing for which she was responsible. Here need for attention, sympathy, pity was so great that the sacrificing of her organs was not too great a price to pay.

We Are Always Praying

What has this to do with prayer? Simply this: "Prayer is the soul's sincere desire, uttered or unexpressed."[3]

We are always praying, in a sense. What we desire at the bottom of our hearts constitutes the prayer, not the words we utter. If I am preoccupied with my own problems but dutifully pray for a sick friend, or world peace, or anything else for that matter, I am virtually wasting my time. I may say, "Lord, bless John in his distress, and heal him if it be your will," but if I am at that moment not particularly concerned about John, my real prayer is, "Lord, I am not especially concerned about John. I am really too preoccupied with problems of my own at the moment." Intensity of desire and the focusing of one's spiritual forces seem essential to effective prayer.

Of course one can pray anywhere—on a bus, at work, washing the dishes, walking on the beach, or in a church. A man told me that he had attended church one morning angry at his wife because she had made them late, as usual. They were late everywhere they went because of her inability to get ready on time. He said, "The service was virtually over before I had calmed down. I spent the entire time being hostile at my wife. But," he added, "I emerged from the church service calmer than when I entered, willing and anxious to establish a better relationship with my wife. Perhaps the service wasn't wasted on me after all, if it helped me become calm again and restored my equanimity."

Whether it be the quiet of a church, the calm serenity of lake or ocean, the stilling effect of great music, or just being alone to look deep within and commune with God— whatever induces this attitude is creative. Some set the mood by reading a few great passages from the Bible or a devotional book. Others are helped by music. Some require the stimulus of corporate worship in a church. It is important to lessen inner tension, and induce a sense of quietness. "In quietness and in trust shall be your strength."[4] "Be still, and know that I am God."[5]

A young married woman wrote me as follows:

Dear Dr. O,
Something will have to be done about not being able to sleep after a Yokefellow meeting. In the process of being wakeful I had a concept. Having a concept is like having a baby. (I assume this from hearsay, of course, not having one.) One wants to share it with those who appreciate such things. Right? I know you like concepts. Ergo:

Why do we pray in the name of Christ? Aside from the fact that we are told to, I mean. What does it really mean? Isn't it because it gives us an image to fix upon?

As you have said many times, "Whatever you visualize you can realize." Somehow the "law of attraction," or "like begets like" seems to be still in force. In this world of symbolism, a symbol is needed.

Practitioners of the healing arts suggest concentrating on health and energy as a means of being healed. So, we pray in the name of Jesus. Why? Because He is our "redeemer"? Because we are "washed in His blood and saved from our sins"? No! Because He was the supreme example of what a totally whole person could be, a human being totally filled with the force of the universe; a Man who exemplified all the universal laws of health, life, joy, abundance and love. He is the symbol of what I *could* be.

When I pray for things, I have to have something in mind to focus on. If I want health, I have to have an example of health. But I don't know what health is. I don't know what emotional maturity is, or what love is. I am praying from a state of non-health, non-maturity, non-love, for something which is unknown to me. I wouldn't know it if it came to me in a flash of blue light with trumpets blowing. I need to know what I'm looking for (not only just to recognize it when it occurs but also to have a focus, a symbol). People around me have health, joy, life, love, in varying degrees, but not to the ultimate degree. And who does have it? Christ! I don't really know Him, but I know about Him, and see His attributes mirrored in others. So, I pray "in His name"; that is, with Him as a focus, a symbol, to channel my awareness.

Yours for bigger and better concepts,
D

Since infinite truth is not to be encompassed by any finite concept, I am sure she does not think that her insight comprises the sum total of all wisdom concerning why we pray "in the name of Jesus," but surely there is a large element of truth in it. " 'If you dwell in me, and my words dwell in you, ask what you will, and you shall have it,' "[6] said Jesus. How does one go about "dwelling in Jesus?" Surely one way would be to envision him as my friend suggested: to focus upon his attributes, to see him as Perfect Love, Perfect Health, Perfect Truth, to see in him "the symbol of what I could be," as she put it.

It is not a question of whether God wills our best. Jesus made it quite clear that God's love envisions the supreme good for us. The problem is how to rid ourselves of our materialistic, fearful, doubting attitudes.

Prayer and Our Relationship with God

There are three basic levels in the Christian life that relate to prayer. The first is *loving to get things from God*. This is the childhood level. I can still recall making my first kite and flying it out in front of the house. A gust of wind sent it toward a tall tree, and I prayed with all the earnestness of my young soul: "O Lord, don't let my kite get caught in that tree!" But it did, and I decided then and there never to trust God again. He hadn't helped me in my hour of need. However, I relented, and prayed again— every time a crisis arose. Who could tell? It might do *some* some good. The magic could work yet if one just prayed hard enough.

I do not doubt that God honors prayers of desperation. He desires to give good things to his children, but to conceive of him primarily as a source of help in a crisis is a very limited and childlike concept. -

We reach the second level of spiritual growth when we *love to serve God*. Ministers who are hard-pressed for workers to keep the church functioning can be pardoned it they appear to stress service to God as the ultimate in spiritual growth. But frantic endeavor, whether in the church kitchen, the men's brotherhood, or organizing a youth program, *can* be a substitute for Christianity. In fact, it is possible for almost any kind of service to God and man to be an unconscious evasion. A true "cop-out," of course, is to want all of the advantages of Christianity and the church without bothering to become involved. The overly fatigued church worker has at least made a contribution, even though on occasion the work may be an unconscious avoidance of God.

The third and final step in spiritual growth is to *love God for himself alone*. At first glance this could seem like a fruitless endeavor. It may suggest abandoning an active and fruitful life to spend endless hours poring over the Bible and devotional literature. To some it conjures up an image of a hooded monk telling his beads before a sputtering candle in some isolated monastery. It's all very well and good for *him* to retreat from the world, and spend his life in pious devotion, but what about my problems, and my endless duties and responsibilities?

This objection is a tricky bit of fast footwork engineered by the inner defense system. Jesus did not suggest withdrawal from the world, or the abdication of our responsibilities. On the contrary, it is recorded that on one occasion Jesus was so busy with the crowds thronging about him that there was not even time to eat.[7] His was not a leisurely life.

He appears to have alternated between periods of intense activity and times of receptivity. He grew weary like any mortal. He frequently took the disciples aside for quiet retreats, then back to the crowded cities and towns.

We can find the principle of his life in one of his most important teachings. He told us to seek first God's kingdom and righteousness; then all these other material things will come to us as a matter of course.[8] They are by-products, and we must not give them priority. God must come first. Life is better that way.

Why We Avoid a Regular Encounter with God

The shattering truth is that we avoid a daily encounter with God because *unconsciously* we fear what he may reveal to us about ourselves, or what he may require of us. It isn't that we do not have the time. A basic, fundamental truth is that we are doing at any given moment what we *prefer* to do. We may not want to get up when the alarm clock goes off, but we prefer it to the alternative. A housekeeper may protest that she is not scrubbing the kitchen floor because she likes to do so, but she prefers it to the alternative of a dirty floor. It is her choice. A man may not like his job, but he prefers it to doing without a paycheck. He is in charge, and chooses the least threatening alternative.

When the twelve-hour day was the rule, and people worked six days a week, and when women churned butter by hand and cooked on a wood range, there might have been some slight truth to the idea that "there just isn't enough time for a daily period of meditation and prayer." Oddly enough, more of those people had what were called "family altars" than today.

No, we avoid God only because we do not like him, or we fear him, which is about the same thing. But more than our service, *God wants our love and fellowship,* and Christ has promised that if we will give priority to this fellowship with the Eternal, life's blessings will come to us as a matter of course. It happens, he said, when we put God first in our lives.

Wanting God for the Wrong Reason

I had a vivid dream one night, in which I was desperately trying to find the whole will of God. I sensed that I had to give up my own will, but I couldn't accomplish it. I was willing, I said to some vague figure with me, to sign a document that I would abandon my will to God, but that emotionally I couldn't do it. It seemed to me that everything, absolutely *everything,* hinged upon my being able to have God's will in my life; but try as I would, I could not surrender my will. The dream involved a seemingly endless struggle.

Finally I was physically and emotionally exhausted, and decided to abandon the struggle. Then I heard myself say, "I give up even *wanting* God!" And at that instant it happened. There was a blaze of glory. Light and joy and life and color exploded within and without. And in the midst of all this I sensed in the back of my mind what the problem had been. Initially, in wanting God, I had secretly been wanting him so that I could *use* him and get his blessings. But when I abandoned this and gave up wanting anything, the answer came. And I sensed at a deep level that God could manifest himself to me as beauty and power and joy and love only when I ceased to want anything at all for myself.

Here is the paradox: to "seek God with all your heart"[9] (an attitude stressed over and over in the Bible), but at the same time to want nothing, not even God. But it ceases to be a paradox when one goes through the first stage of wanting him with all of one's being, then through the second stage of realizing that even in this desire there are selfish motives, and then to the third stage of abandoning even the desire for God so that he can manifest himself. This is the only true surrender to the will of God; and surprisingly, when you surrender your will totally to God, it is handed back. You are still in charge! Sadly enough, the experience must be gone through again and again, for being human we keep taking our wills back. The Apostle Paul said, "I die daily."[10] I take this to mean that every day he had to resurrender his will, and "die" to self-interest.

Years after the dream in which I gave up wanting God, I had another in which I was one of a vast throng of people, all of whom wore crowns. My crown seemed to symbolize that I was the king of my own inner kingdom. But there was so much beauty and joy apparent over to my left that I felt a need to join it. I sensed that in order to do so I would have to abandon my own identity, but it seemed a small price to pay if I could experience what I perceived there.

I took off my crown and handed it to some nameless, faceless individual who stood at the entrance to the place where all the joy and beauty were in evidence. Gently he handed it back, and I wept, for when I put it back on again I still had my humanity, my problems, and all of the innumerable decisions to make which go along with being a human with an identity. The implication was clear: "You cannot abdicate. You are the king of your own kingdom, the god of your inner world. You are in charge." And I hadn't wanted to be in charge. I had sought to give up and let God run things without my having to assume responsibility for my own actions.

Prayer, then, involves not only a matter of attitudes and one's whole spiritual and emotional nature, but the willingness to assume responsibility for one's life and actions, while wanting God's glorious, wonderful will for ourselves and others.

Being Out of Harmony

Much prayer seems to be "praying *to* the problem," rather than about the fundamental problem itself. For instance, a person with rheumatoid arthritis, or ulcers, or asthma, or any of a hundred other physical symptoms will probably get worse if he prays for a healing of the symptom. Most physical illnesses are simply a physical manifestation of an emotional or spiritual disharmony. "O God, relieve me of the pain, the discomfort," one prays over and over. The symptom—the pain—is brought into focus, rather than God and his power.

That this is all wrong is taught clearly by Jesus. A paraphrase of Matthew 6:3 would go like this: "You have it all backwards. You worry about what you are going to wear, or eat, or drink. You are focusing upon the *problem*. The first thing to do is seek God's will, and get into perfect harmony with it, and everything else will fall into place as a matter of course."

There is perfect harmony in God's realm, the kingdom of heaven. He desires that we shall have this harmony in our lives, but the only way it can happen is to abandon the practice of focusing upon the problem. Focus upon the goodness of God, the harmony which he desires to bring into our lives and relationships. Get to the root of the problem, which is that we are out of harmony with God's glorious will.

It's very easy to get out of harmony, and be caught up in false values. A journalist went to interview Dr. J. B. Phillips, in England.[11] He found him to be open, friendly and relaxed; but almost from the outset Dr. Phillips began to talk, not about his recent illness, but about his spiritual illness.

He said that during the closing days of the war he had found that young people had no interest in the King James translation of the Bible. Consequently he did a translation of part of the New Testament which he entitled *Letters to Young Churches*. It was an instant sensation, and sold by the millions in both England and the United States. He was almost immediately besieged with invitations to speak. He traveled widely and his correspondence became enormous. He was suddenly a great success, and he liked it. He was famous, known around the world.

As he described it, he was no longer an ordinary human being. "I was in danger of becoming a kind of super-Christian. Everything I wrote or said had to be better than the last. My image grew until it was so unlike me that I could no longer live with it. Yet the thought of destroying (this false image) was terrifying."

His creativity ceased, and he could no longer write. Irrational fears swept over him. "It was the dark night of the soul for me," he said. The problem was how to abandon this false image which had grown up, and become his true self.

A friend of his, C. S. Lewis, who had written many outstanding books, had died in 1963. One night Dr. Phillips was sitting watching TV. In a chair nearby C. S. Lewis appeared, looking ruddy, healthy, and very much alive. Lewis said, "It's not so hard as you think, you know."

What wasn't so hard? Finally it dawned on him. "It's not so hard to give up the false self as you think." Like many another, Dr. Phillips had permitted the world's values to woo him away from his real self. Lewis added, "It is a glorious thing to be yourself!"

When we hold false values, we are out of harmony with the exquisite perfection of God's universe. Egocentricity is the most subtle sin of all. It involves pride, the father of all sins. In that spiritual condition prayer becomes either meaningless or futile. For effective prayer hinges upon our being our real selves.

The church which I once served was on a main highway, and innumerable itinerants dropped in for a handout. All wanted a night's lodging, or transportation to the next stop where everything was going to be wonderful. One who visited me turned out to be an ex-minister. He was hungry, broke and desperate. He produced evidence of having served a number of rather large churches.

I asked him what had happened. He told me how his

denomination had let him down, how the members of his last church had betrayed him. His friends had abandoned him. His seminary was partly to blame, as were his parents, society and everyone else.

What does one do, I thought, in a half-hour conference—or for that matter a day-long conference—with a man who blames everyone but himself? At no point could he sense that there might be something wrong with his attitude. I doubted being able in a brief time, if ever, to change his fundamental attitude toward life. The best I could do was to express interest, give him enough money for food and lodging, and ask if he cared to come back for further discussion about his future. He had no interest in the latter, but was mildly grateful for the money.

It seems almost simplistic to say it, but it needs to be said: if your attitude is wrong, nothing will be right. If your attitude is right, everything else will turn out satisfactorily in the end.

This bears on prayer, because if we try to pray with a wrong attitude, we are wasting time. Jesus underscored this in the single comment he made after giving the Lord's Prayer to the disciples. " 'For if you forgive others the wrongs they have done, your heavenly Father will also forgive you; but if you do not forgive others, then the wrongs you have done will not be forgiven by your Father.' "[12] By his very nature, God cannot give to me what I am unwilling to give to another.

Four Basic Principles Concerning Prayer

Thus we come to some basic, fundamental principles involved in effective prayer:

First, honesty with God, with others, and with oneself is the all-essential first step. And self-honesty is not easy. We each have a vested interest in preserving some illusions about ourselves and our motives. This is one reason a sharing group is helpful in spiritual growth. After participating in a Yokefellow group for six months or so a woman said, "I joined this group in the hope that my husband would get some help from it. I came along just to be sure he did. Now I have discovered a dozen areas of my own life that need to be cleared up. I thought he was the whole problem. It's both of us. My needs were as great as his."

Second, while God is quite capable of answering "crisis prayers" for people who have neglected prayer and worship, we are often unable to believe it at a deep level, simply because we do not feel worthy. "Why should God do anything for me now, when I never pray unless I am in some kind of a jam?" as one man expressed it. We serve our own interests best by maintaining some regular pattern of worship, prayer and meditation. "Weeds grow up and choke the unused path," as an old proverb has it.

Third, prayer must not be limited to supplication. Asking for help or guidance can certainly be a part of prayer, but prayer solely for "things" puts us in the position of an itinerant panhandler, who comes asking for assistance only when in dire distress. At its best prayer involves expressions of gratitude, adoration, and praise to God, and communion with him; being willing to forgive others; opening the self to God's cleansing and forgiveness; intercessory prayer for others; and the seeking of God's whole will for one's life.

Fourth, intercessory prayer is an expression of our concern that God's will shall be done for others, as well as for ourselves. I am often asked, "Does it do any good to pray for others? If so, how does it work?" I don't know precisely how it works, but surely it should be as effective to pray for another as to pray for oneself. I need not know the divine mechanism involved, any more than I must understand the electronic mysteries involved in television broadcasting and reception in order to appreciate a TV program.

Prayer and Faith

In 1878 the French Academy of Sciences met to examine Thomas Edison's phonograph. After listening for a bit, one famous French scientist shouted, "Wretch! We are not to be made dupes of by a ventriloquist!"

Sir William Barrett recorded a similar reaction to Alexander Graham Bell's telephone. He wrote, "I happened to be staying in Edinburgh with that famous physicist, Professor Tait, when news of Bell's invention of the telephone came to us by cable. I asked Tait what he thought of it. He replied, 'It is all humbug, for such a discovery is physically impossible.'"

Edison's discovery of the principle of the incandescent

light provoked a reaction from a world-renowned scientist: "It is obviously a fraud, because such a thing violates a basic principle of physics. There can be no light without combustion, and combustion cannot take place in a vacuum." He had apparently never seen a firefly, much less Edison's new incandescent light bulb. His mind was made up.

I am not disposed to doubt what man may accomplish, as he discovers new aspects of God's creation. Much less do I doubt the power of God. Jesus once said to the Twelve, " 'If you have faith no bigger even than a mustard-seed, you will say to this mountain, "Move from here to there!" and it will move; nothing will prove impossible to you.' "[13]

Place a prism on the window sill and let it break up the invisible rays of the sun into their component elements. All of the primary colors are now visible in a blaze of glory. At one end are the red or heat rays; at the other are the ultra-violet or purple rays. The red rays are vibrating quite slowly. The rays at the other end of the spectrum vibrate at an incredible speed. But on beyond the visible colors there are other hues not visible to the imperfect human eye. We know they are there because they have been photographed with film much more sensitive than the human eye.

Beyond the range of the keenest human ear there are ultrasonic sound waves, too rapid to be perceived by any human. And outside the range of our rather dull five senses there are millions of things transpiring which we accept "on faith" in the scientists who report that they have sensed or perceived them. If I can believe the testimony of a fallible scientist (and scientists have often been proven wrong), surely I have no basis for doubting Jesus. Trusting and believing him is no greater an act of faith than accepting blindly the statement of a physicist that matter consists chiefly if not entirely of energy, that there are sound and light waves beyond my power to perceive them, and that it is possible to measure the distance between earth and the moon to within a few feet.

A father brought his son to Jesus to be healed. " 'If it is at all possible for you, take pity upon us and help us,' " he said.

" 'If it is possible!' said Jesus. 'Everything is possible to one who has faith.' 'I have faith,' cried the boy's father; 'help me where faith falls short.' "[14]

Jesus' blanket statement that "everything is possible to one who has faith" is a challenge to our doubt-ridden minds. Then the question arises, "How does one acquire such faith?" To begin with, one does not acquire deep faith in a crisis, any more than a farmer gathers a harvest if he has not diligently plowed, harrowed, planted, and cultivated his fields. I can have virtually anything if I desire it with sufficient intensity. I say "virtually" because there are certain limitations imposed by circumstances. For instance, I doubt that I could become an astronaut or an orchestra conductor. Perhaps I am limiting God in saying so; but of course my very doubt renders me incapable of achieving those goals, even if it were theoretically possible. And since I have not the slightest desire to be any of those things, it becomes literally impossible.

But I am convinced that Jesus was stating a literal truth when he declared that anything is possible to one who believes. "Take what you want and pay for it," goes an old Spanish proverb. If you want faith sufficiently, you can have it. You will pay for it in terms of discipline, focusing your attention upon this one goal almost to the exclusion of all others. It will need to be given priority.

But, as Meister Eckhart phrases it, "If you want God only, you may have all else beside." It will be worth whatever it costs.

You can have as much of God as you want. You're in charge.

7.

Are You Growing?

"It's hard to do the will of God,
but it's hell if you don't."
—C. GILLETTE

"The unexamined life is not
worth living."

—SOCRATES

A DEEP sea diver encased in full diving regalia, and linked by air hose and communication system to the ship two hundred feet above him, was exploring a sunken vessel. Suddenly over his earphones came an anguished cry from the ship overhead: "Come up at once! The ship is sinking!"

This understandable ambivalence is similar to that of the man with an aching tooth who is desperately afraid of dentists. We are all in a double bind. We are anxious to be known, but fearful of revealing ourselves, lest we be rejected. We are poised on the razor's edge, as it were, wistfully longing for others to manifest a deep interest in us, yet frightened lest our secrets be discovered. Anything which can tip the scales in favor of revealing ourselves is to be welcomed.

A cartoon depicts a tiny bug looking up at a praying mantis asking, "What kind of an insect are you?" "I'm a praying mantis," is the reply.

"That's ridiculous! Insects don't pray."

The praying mantis seizes the hapless bug by the neck

109

and squeezes. The bug rolls his eyes frantically heavenward and begins, "Our Father who art in Heaven . . ."

The cartoonist is pointing out an inescapable truth. Nothing motivates us so much as pain, or some powerful threat to our well-being. We make no significant change in our personalities or our life situation except as the result of pain, or the threat of a great loss.

You have a choice, since you alone are in charge of making the decisions governing your life. If you are lonely, or unhappy and frustrated; if you are not receiving as much love and understanding as you would like; if life is not providing adequate fulfillment for you, you have at least two major alternatives.

One, you can remain imprisoned within the gray castle of your loneliness. This way you run little or no risk of rejection. You can withdraw from life into the safety of your walled castle.

Two, you can decide to run the risk of possible hurt or rejection by letting others get to know you. Naturally it is not advisable to open up to just anyone. We need to screen our friends and confidants in order to find people who are on our wavelength.

So, you are in charge of whether you will remain imprisoned within your pain and loneliness, or whether you will run the risk of being known.

For some, this latter alternative may mean professional counseling, or sharing on a regular basis with a minister with whom you relate well, and whom you trust. Others find it in a sharing group.

Growth in Groups

Rose was thirty-seven, married and dully miserable, although no one would have guessed it. Even she was unaware of how unhappy she was, because she had buried her feelings very deeply. She simply could not allow herself to feel, except superficially.

Hers was more the dull throb of frustration than the sharp stab of a crisis. She and her husband had a most unsatisfying relationship, but neither knew what to do about it. She had a few sessions with a psychiatrist which, she said, only made her more frustrated.

Eventually Rose asked for an appointment and inquired about joining a Yokefellow group. She wanted to know if she could visit a few times to see how she liked it. "No," I replied. "One does not visit a Yokefellow group. You join and attend for at least three months. By that time you will know whether you can derive benefit from the experience."

"What if my husband won't come?"

"Then you can attend alone, though it would be better if he would come with you. However, your growth can precipitate a change in your relationship. You must be prepared, though, for the possibility that significant growth on your part could make him angry."

Rose was willing to take the chance. She joined a group of nine other persons who had been meeting together for some time. It was an "open ended" group. When someone dropped out a new member was added. Once a year the group took a "spiritual growth inventory," consisting of a standardized psychological test, with a feedback system of eleven evaluation slips in sealed envelopes. These were handed out every two weeks by the leader.

Rose was frankly terrified of the whole thing. The group members had learned to express their feelings, and she was desperately afraid of any display of emotion. Whether it was anger or love, Rose was equally embarrassed. She had learned as a child, by observing her emotionally controlled parents, that feelings were never to be expressed.

When the first slip was handed out, Rose's hand trembled as she opened her envelope. What horrible secret, what ancient skeleton, would be revealed? What form of moral depravity or spiritual deficiency would be discovered?

I watched the expression on her face as others read their slips; her anxiety changed to relief. Finally the leader turned to her and said, "Rose, there is nothing mandatory about reading your slip here in the group. You can take it home and sleep on it if you prefer."

"No, I'll read it. At first I wondered if I might be some sort of psychological misfit when I read this, but two others in the group had similar ones, so maybe I'm not too much worse off than the rest of you. Here goes:

FEAR OF EMOTIONS

This area of the test shows that you are excessively afraid of your feelings. This can cause a lack of deep emotional response in your life, and cause you to blame yourself for continually making the same mistakes. You can experience life more fully as you begin to practice honesty about your feelings, thus learning to be aware of them. Accept your emotions. They are all valid.

SUGGESTIONS: This week let the group help you with your fear. As you strive for honesty with your feelings, you will see that others accept you regardless of the feelings you show. In this way you can become aware of your feelings, and accept them as your fear diminishes. This week read chapter five in *Prayer Can Change Your Life,* as you ask yourself what it is that you fear. This will help you learn to accept your feelings, not as ideal, but as real and valid.

Do not be afraid to tell God precisely how you feel. He knows anyway, and he understands:

"When you can let God take you by the hand and lead you into that corner of your life where you fear to venture, you can be free."

Rose finished reading and looked up thoughtfully. "It's all true. I'm scared spitless of my feelings. My father was an alcoholic, and his anger was frightening when he was drunk. Mother repressed all of her feelings in order not to let herself feel how terribly trapped she was. My sisters and I learned to keep quiet and out of sight."

"That's what *happened,* Rose," someone said, "but tell us how you *felt* when your father came home drunk."

"Just terrified! I can feel myself getting anxious right now thinking about it. When he was sober, he was delightful. But when he was drinking, he'd beat my mother. I never knew why she didn't leave him."

"What do you feel right now, Rose?" a group member asked.

"A mixture of emotions. I loved my father, but I was scared to death of him."

"I understand, but what are you feeling *this moment?*"

"As though I'd like to pound him right into the ground.

I can see his ugly, drunken face, and I'd like to punch him, kill him . . . oh . . . that's a terrible thing to say!"

"Don't sit in judgment on your feelings, Rose," the leader said. "Feelings are always valid. You feel whatever you feel. You sounded more like a real person when you told us what you'd like to do to your father. It was an honest feeling."

"You mean it's all right to feel hate and anger? I thought we were supposed to love one another. 'Honor your father and mother,' and all that sort of thing. I've always felt guilty about hating my parents."

"Jesus got angry on occasion," someone said, "and so do we all. We can handle our anger better if we face it. Rose, go on and tell us about your feelings. What did you feel about your mother?"

"She was meek and mousy. Why she put up with that sort of abuse for forty years I'll never know."

"How does it make you *feel?*"

"Hostile. Angry. Bitter. And I feel pity for her, too, because she took so much abuse. Maybe she didn't know how to get out of the mess. Say! Come to think of it, I feel angry at myself for putting up with so much from my own husband. I've buried my feelings and pretended, and been phony, just to keep him from exploding. I can't stand criticism. And if I don't perform to suit him, he tells me about it with brutal frankness. Then if I offer the slightest criticism of him, he tells me I don't love him, and he sulks for days on end."

"What do you feel right now?"

"Terrible! I'd like to hit him, scream at him, shout at him, but nice girls don't do that, especially nice Christian girls. But I'd like to, just the same. Isn't that awful?" She looked around the circle to see how much rejection she was going to receive.

"Rose, I felt the same way for years about my husband, and he was as angry and frustrated as I was. Carl is sitting over there looking smug and self-satisfied. And in a way he has a right to feel smug. I dragged him here to this group so he could get some help. Then I found that I needed changing as much as he did. I was as neurotic and selfish as he was. Both of us have grown enormously. We can communicate now, after fourteen years of married frustration."

"But my husband won't come to a group like this. He thinks he's perfect. I'm the one who's sick, according to him."

"You are the only person you can change, but when you change, others around you tend to change in reaction to the 'new' you."

George spoke up. "I haven't read my slip yet. It's so painfully true, and possibly true of Rose's husband. Let me read it and see if she gets any insight from it:

OVER-COMPENSATION

You have a tendency to try to appear more confident than you actually feel, in order to compensate for feelings of inadequacy or weakness. This is a very normal tendency, but one which can cause strain. Apparently you developed a standard of behavior during your early life which was that of a "strong person." Until you are able to accept yourself with both your strengths and your weaknesses, you will be forcing something which you do not feel. Seek with patience to accept yourself as you are.

To increase your self-confidence, during the next two weeks make up a list of your virtues and your strengths. List every good impulse and every positive attribute you possess. Add to your list as new items suggest themselves. Focus on this daily.

For a better picture of yourself, read pages 227–30 in *Prayer Can Change Your Life*, and pages sixty to seventy-eight. Also read chapters eleven and twelve. Then read chapter four in *The Art of Understanding Yourself*. The answer to your problems, like the kingdom of heaven, is within you. You will discover your true source of inner strength as you spend time alone with God and your own soul daily.

George was silent for a few moments, thinking. "It's all true, every bit of it. I've known it vaguely all my life. I feel inadequate, a sense of diffused inferiority. I don't *think* I'm inferior, but I feel that way, and I don't know why. I have always succeeded in everything I've undertaken, yet I still feel unworthy, or inferior, as though I didn't quite measure up."

114

Someone asked, "Did your parents set abnormally high standards for you?"

"Gosh, yes! Nothing I ever did won my parents' approval, as I look back on it now. At the time I was vaguely unhappy and didn't know why. If I got Bs and Cs, they should have been all As and Bs. When I made that, then I was given to understand that I could make all As if I tried harder. When I achieved that one year, they had new goals for me. My posture was bad. My table manners were atrocious. I could be more polite, keep my room neater, do more around the house. I got no input of approval; they just kept setting the standards higher and higher. I never made it. I probably never will make it, because I have some irrational perfectionistic standards imprinted on my brain."

"What are you feeling right now?"

"Angry, frustrated, and guilty because I know in my head that my parents were wonderful people. I hate criticizing them; yet I know that all my hangups originated with them, just as my kids' hangups all come from my perfectionism. Maybe this is the meaning of original sin—a kind of corporate guilt we pass on from generation to generation. But I feel guilty for having transmitted it to my children. I have been demanding and critical, just as my father was. I am feeling self-hate right now, for my own inept, bungling handling of my kids."

"What could you do to be released from this perfectionistic approach to life?" the leader asked.

"Well, first of all I could let up on my kids; stop demanding so much. I could begin by treating them the way I would like to have been treated by my father."

"How's that?"

"Well, I would like to have had more positive input. More approval. As it was, I felt that I got twenty criticisms for every fragment of approval. After I got out of school and succeeded pretty well in my first job, my father offered some warm approval. I heard him, but it didn't register. The feeling was, 'It's too late, Dad. I needed that a long time ago. I made it on my own without your help. Your acceptance is about twenty years too late.' He often expressed pride in my achievements after that, but I could never accept it. It didn't matter one way or another whether he approved or not. I had shut him out long before."

"How do you feel when you say that?"

"Sad. As though I want to cry, both for him and for that kid who wanted some approval."

"Why don't you?"

"It isn't manly. But I'm crying inside. It's my inner child of five or seven or ten who's crying right now." He took out a handkerchief and wiped his eyes.

A woman next to him put her arm around him and said, "George, I'm feeling a lot for that kid. I could cry with you, partly because I had some of that same treatment. I have a lot of unshed tears in me, and some day they're going to come out."

"I think," said one of the men, "that our educational system is at fault, and . . ."

"Hold it, Ted," the leader interrupted. "You were about to give us a great intellectual concept. Most of us would agree with you perhaps, but this is a 'feeling group.' The 'think group' met last night. I wonder if you were becoming intellectual in order to avoid something."

"Well, as a matter of fact I suppose I was. My slip is headed 'Separation of Intellect and Emotions.' Want me to read it?"

"Go ahead."

"OK. Here goes. I don't like it, but it rings a bell."

SEPARATION OF INTELLECT AND EMOTION

You feelings and thinking are not working harmoniously, as evidenced by the fact that you have labeled some of your feelings as "bad" or "sinful." Thus you cannot accept them. When we accept feelings, we do not thereby give approval. We simply admit that they are there, and accept them as a fact to be dealt with. The danger in separating feelings from intellect is that in time we may suffer from anxieties, nervous tension, and occasional feelings of panic. These are simply warnings to us to accept ourselves. We cannot abandon to God feelings which we deny. The group can help you to accept yourself, if you are honest with them.

List all the thoughts and feelings which you consider "bad," surrendering them, one by one, to God. Then list everything for which you are grateful, including the good things about yourself. Thank God for them, and let Him worry about the rest. Read chapters one through four in Ephesians (RSV or Phillips' translation), noting all the promises and gifts which are yours as a loved and accepted child of God. Then read chapter six in *The Art of Understanding Yourself*.

During the daily quiet time, you will learn to cope with these discoveries about yourself.

God condemns no one who begins, where he is, to walk toward the light. Though we fall a thousand times, his love forgives. Be no harder on yourself than God is.

Ted pondered this for a moment, then said, "What's that all about? I do have some anxiety and tension, but so does everyone else. I'm no intellectual, yet this speaks of separating my intellect from my emotions. What does it mean?"

"Just what it says," said someone. "You have avoided your feelings, denied them, buried them, and relied on your intellect almost solely. You have tended to deny that you have feelings, because you are afraid of them."

"I'll say he is," said his wife. "Any time I want to get down to a feeling level, he begins with a lecture, or at least a monologue, dealing with facts and concepts. By the time he is finished I am either so angry or frustrated or bored that I think, 'Oh, the hell with it.' And I don't try again for maybe a week or a month. Then I get the same calm intellectual approach."

"What's wrong with that?" Ted asked. "Is thinking such a great sin?"

"No," responded one of the women, "but it is a great sin to cut yourself off from your feelings, as you have done. You shut Grace out when you deal only with cool concepts. And you shut the rest of us out. I don't really know you, though you've been in the group for six months. All I know is what you think, and that's not knowing you. What do you feel, Ted? Do you ever feel anger, love, frustration, jealousy, fear, guilt, inferiority, like the rest of mankind; or are you all alone on your Mount Olympus with your great sanitary, hygienic thoughts?"

"Oh, go to hell, Mary Lou," he grinned. "I get the message. Grace has been saying the same thing from the first day we were married. The truth is, I am afraid of my feelings, because whenever I expressed a feeling as a kid I got smacked down. I learned to cut my feelings off. I got along better when I was like my Dad. He was an unfeeling, calm, controlled person. I suppose I absorbed some of his personality traits just by osmosis."

"You're talking *about* your feelings, but I have not heard you express a true feeling since you joined the group," one of the men said. "What are you feeling this moment, as you think of that kid whose spontaneity was squashed. How does it make you feel to know that your capacity for joy, compassion, love, and all the other feelings, was trampled, so that you became a thinking machine unable to feel anything deeply? A kid is normally spontaneously angry or happy, or curious, or affectionate. And you had to suppress all these God-given emotions just to survive. How does that make you feel?"

"I don't feel much of anything. I've lived too long on the level of the intellect. Maybe my feelings are all dead."

One of the women went over and sat on the floor at his feet, took hold of his hand, and said, "Ted, close your eyes a moment. Now feel your way back to the time when you were five or six or seven. See your calm, unemotional dad, and your undemonstrative mother. You're a kid now, and you need something desperately. Look at them. What is it that you *want* from them. Don't think. *Feel!"*

Ted sat in silence for a moment, then in a soft voice he said, "I want to be held, loved. I can't remember ever being held." He sat, eyes closed, feeling the loneliness of his childhood.

The leader motioned to several in the group and they stood in the center of the circle. The woman at Ted's feet stood up and said, "Ted, keep your eyes closed. I'm going to lead you into a little circle of love." She took his hand and led him to the center of the circle where four or five stood waiting. They gathered around him, and enclosed him in a warm, loving embrace. They stood there in silence for several minutes. They were loving and holding Ted's inner child of the past. At first he was rigid and tense. But gradually he relaxed and let himself feel their love. At a feeling level he was six or eight years old, or younger. Someone murmured, "Relax, Ted. Let go. Let us love you."

Finally they separated in silence, and Ted sat down. He

wiped his eyes. "Lord, that felt good! I felt like crying buckets. I guess those were the unshed tears I have never been able to let out. But I can feel them inside."

One of the women in the circle was weeping silently. Someone handed her some Kleenex. The group waited. Finally she said, "I was crying for Ted, and for another kid. Me. I was the first child in the family, and I suppose I developed a princess syndrome. When my little brother was born, I felt totally abandoned. No one paid any attention to me. It seemed to me that everyone turned their full attention on my baby brother. I pretended to love him, but I could have thrown him out the window. I wanted to get rid of him and win back some of the love I had lost. I don't recall ever feeling loved again. Boys were 'better.' I didn't know just how, but I got that message. I did everything to get their love. Good grades, total compliance. That didn't do it, so I tried another route. I became rebellious. That got to them.

"Finally at fifteen I got pregnant. That *really* got their attention! I wasn't consciously aware that I was frantically trying to get love, or attention, and I'm sure I didn't get pregnant intentionally to punish them; but now I can see that I was driven by a need to get attention, and at the same time to punish them for ignoring me. Believe me, I got plenty of attention, most of it negative. But even that, and the scandal, was better than being ignored. So, when Ted was standing there letting himself feel loved, I wanted to be there, too, because this group represents my family. Good grief, I have felt more love in this group than I ever got from my family after my kid brother came along. In fact, this *is* my family."

The leader said, "It's about time to close. Suppose we gather in a tight circle, with Gwen in the middle. We'll hold her, in love." Gwen let herself be surrounded and held. With eyes closed, in silence, the group members loved Gwen, and each other.

The leader said, "Tell us what you are feeling, if you wish."

Someone said, "I feel loved. Giving and receiving love is what it's all about."

"Love is of God," another said. "He who does not know love does not know God. I feel God in our midst."

"I feel like I belong to a family, at last, where I am loved no matter what I do or say."

"I feel unconditional acceptance for the first time in my life. This group is my church and my family."

The leader closed with a simple, one-sentence prayer. The group members stood around for another twenty minutes talking, visiting, enjoying each other. They had been part of a loving fellowship for two and a half hours.

Growth Can Be Painful

The closed, or static personality is one that has ceased to grow. Growth is painful, or at least it involves effort and stress. Many people settle for the status quo rather than face the prospect of change and growth. It is easier to demand that others around us conform to our desires than to admit to our own deficiencies.

After a dozen or more counseling sessions with Paul and Mary, I began to have serious doubts as to whether their marriage could survive. It was the second marriage for each of them. Mary was desperately anxious to make this one work.

One of her major complaints was that Paul was undependable. He would promise to phone and let her know when he was going to be delayed. In one instance, typical of scores, he phoned from another city to say that he would be home on a certain flight. She met the plane. No Paul. She finally went home and waited for a phone call which never came. Two days later he showed up as if nothing had happened. This sort of conduct triggered great anxiety in her. She did not seek to control his actions, but did feel a need to know when he would come home.

When faced with this in our sessions, Paul would go into a rage. Defensively he would shout that he had no intention of ever letting any woman control his destiny. His tirades would go on at considerable length while Mary managed to keep reasonably calm.

Nothing I could say to Paul made any difference. It was as if he were deaf, or uncomprehending. Actually, he had simply built his defenses, organized his life, and expected everyone else to conform and accept him as he was. He showed not the slightest willingness to compromise, or to meet his wife's needs.

120

Mary had another complaint. Paul insisted on showing her how to run her kitchen. He even angrily insisted that the way she sliced onions was all wrong. They had a fearful row over that one. He thought nothing of pointing out all of her defects in the presence of friends and visitors.

Finally Mary came in alone one day. "Do you really think there is any hope for this marriage?" she asked.

"Not unless you have the ego, strength, and resilience to put up with his rages and all of the other things that are driving you up the wall."

"You mean he isn't going to change?"

"Well, so far I have not seen the slightest indication that he is willing to change one iota. I do not rule out a miracle of divine grace, for they sometimes occur. But as of now, I see no reason for you to continue seeing me. However, you can tell him quietly what your limits are. Let him know that you are not making any demands that he change, but that you cannot and will not endure certain things. Set your limits. If he cares to try to meet your basic needs, then you can both come back. Otherwise, I would give it up as hopeless."

The next day she phoned for an appointment. A few days later they both came in. He looked more thoughtful than I had ever seen him. In fact, he was as gentle as a lamb. For the first time he didn't go into a towering, irrational rage.

"Mary has shared some important needs of hers," he said humbly, "and I want to find out how I can go about meeting them. I can see where I've been wrong. I'm going to have to change if our relationship is to last. Tell me how I can go about it."

We spent the rest of the hour on this one point. Mary was not a demanding person, but she did have some reasonable, normal needs. He was listening for the first time. "I may not be able to make a go of it one hundred percent of the time at first, but I can start," he said. "I can see where I've been wrong."

I have not the faintest idea what took place in his mind when she calmly set her limits. The reaction I would have predicted, based on previous performance, would have been rage and violent profanity.

As they were leaving, a shadow of doubt crossed my mind. I half-wondered if Paul was giving both of us a snow job. Almost as if he read my mind, he said, "Now look, I can't do this on my own. I'm going to need more help. We'll both need to see you on a regular basis, in order to make this work."

Many a husband or wife has made demands, threats, and used all of the other standard manipulative devices, in an effort to stir the other. Mary simply stated her limits. If he felt unable to meet them, she was through as of that moment. He did not perceive this as an ultimatum, or a threat, which it was not. He simply saw what he had to lose if he didn't express some willingness to change his attitude.

I had mistakenly classified Paul as a closed personality, someone totally unwilling to change. He turned out to be far more open than I could have guessed. His change of attitude was genuine as evidenced by the greatly improved marriage relationship.

William James of Harvard, founder of modern psychology, affirms that the average person uses no more than 10 percent of his mental capacity. Fear, pride, and childhood programming probably account for the fact that we use such a small proportion of our potential.

It seems almost incredible that Jesus would have chosen those twelve inept, untrained, spiritually dull men to provide the heart and core of his movement. Apparently he wanted to demonstrate what God could accomplish through very ordinary human beings. To them he entrusted the entire future of the little fellowship. Yet, in three hundred years the Christian movement had captured the Roman empire spiritually, and grew faster than at any time since.

It was a living demonstration of the fact that "in everything God works . . . with those who love him."[1]

To be open to his will is to be open to his power. He has no desire to control you, but he does want to channel his love and power and guidance through you. You and you alone are in charge of whether you will be an open or closed personality, growing or static.

8.

How to Become a Real Person

> "He who looks back dies of remorse."
>
> —ANONYMOUS

IN ENGLAND I finally found what I had been searching for. For many years I had, for some vague reason, wanted a large pair of brass scales. I had never given much thought as to the reason for this particular desire. In fact, I had a vested interest in not examining the real motive.

In Athens, browsing in antique shops, I found myself passing up some ancient artifacts, which I love, and searching for a pair of scales. On the island of Crete, and later in Rhodes, I examined a dozen or more in various shops. I almost bought one pair, but for some obscure reason I didn't, though some were reasonably priced. Later I realized that it was because they were new. I wanted an *old* pair, though I was not aware of the reason at the time.

Finally in a London antique shop I found a beautiful pair guaranteed to be at least a hundred years old. They cost roughly three times as much as a modern set I had looked at in Rhodes, but the price was not too important. I "needed" that particular ornamental pair of scales for my office.

I placed them on top of my stereo set, which is the only place in my office where they looked right. It made it awkward to open the top of the stereo, but that seemed unimportant when I discovered that it was precisely the spot where they looked best.

Oddly enough they were quite close to my desk, where I could see them easily. Rather compulsively I finally got them balanced perfectly. They actually looked better, artistically, when not so well balanced, but I needed to have them balanced *evenly*. Having achieved the perfect balance by weighting one side slightly, I sat back and studied them. For the first time I let myself discover the real reason for my semi-compulsive search for a beautiful pair of brass scales.

In the environment in which I was reared there was a great emphasis upon good and bad, right and wrong. Everything was black or white—no grays. People were either good or bad, actions were either right or wrong. There was no middle ground.

The small church which our family attended consisted of the "good" people of the community. "Bad" people stayed home or went fishing, and everyone knew that fishing on Sunday was wicked. Most of the ministers, and all of the evangelists—and there were scores of them—made it their business to make me feel as guilty as possible. God knows I was already very guilty, but on Sunday I became even more so. Or at least I *felt* more guilty. In fact I felt guilty about almost everything.

God was a God of justice, not mercy. I spent a great deal of time dwelling on what was going to happen on judgment day, when the books were opened, and the secrets of all hearts revealed. *The scales must balance!*

Oh, the scales! Justice, equity, righteousness, perfection. As I studied my new acquisition and observed how perfectly balanced they were, it all came back to me. So *that* was the source of my compulsion to have a beautiful pair of brass scales, and get them perfectly balanced. Now I knew why they had to be old; because the memories were old. The scars of false guilt (plus a lot of real guilt) were as old as I was.

For many years I had known intellectually about the God of mercy, who forgives instantly and gladly when we confess. I knew all of the scriptures about divine forgiveness, and had quoted them a thousand times to other people. I knew it in my head, that is. Unfortunately head knowledge has little to do with feelings. There is no direct communication between intellectual knowledge and feelings.

Nothing Is Ever Completely Forgotten

Unfortunately, time does not diminish guilt. The memory may fade. The event may even be "forgotten"—that is, stored in the unconscious mind, repressed—but very real. But one of the contributions made by Freud was his discovery that memories are not simply "forgotten," or put into dead storage like an old trunk stored in the basement. A trunk full of ancient photographs, letters and assorted junk does no damage in the basement; but *every thought, emotion, and event has some effect upon the personality, either positive or negative.*

Dr. Hans Selye of Canada is the father of the stress theory.[1] In essence it is his contention, now widely accepted in medical circles, that stress is the origin of all illness, either physical or mental. Stress may result from excessive fatigue, from continued and persistent overwork; or it may be caused by negative emotions—by fear, anxiety, guilt, hate, jealousy. No amount of rationalization diminishes guilt, for the unconscious mind does not accept a rationalization, no matter how clever. The illness of today may result from accumulated stresses over a period of five or fifty years.

One may line up a dozen or a hundred friends to verify the fact that he was right in his quarrel with someone, but the inner judicial system is not interested in counting votes. It registers only the emotion of anger, or fear, or guilt.

A young married woman came to me for counseling. There was no outward evidence of her inner turmoil. The immediate problem she shared had to do with the fact that she was a "recovered" alcoholic, and that there were some marital problems which needed to be resolved.

In the course of her counseling I put her in a Yokefellow group which was in the process of taking a spiritual growth inventory, consisting of a standardized psychological test. One of the fifteen areas covered by the test has to do with self-abasement. When she received the weekly evaluation slip on this subject, she was happy to discover that she scored very low in this area. I looked up her exact score later. It was seven, far below the average, of course. It made her happy to think that she did not experience undue self-rejection, and felt no need to accuse herself. In a private session I told her that there was something wrong. She had denied some of her real feelings. They were so deeply repressed that she was out of touch with her true emotions.

"Your excessive drinking was an escape for something. Would you care to tell me what it was?" There was a long pause. Then the full story came out. She had been sexually promiscuous for many years. However, she stated that she felt no guilt over that part of her life now that she was married.

I said, "You buried your guilt, and tried to repress the memories because they were too painful. Your alcoholism was only a symptom of the real problem."

"But that's all in the past," she said. "It's ended. Don't you teach that God forgives, and that we should accept his forgiveness?"

"Quite right," I replied, "but you haven't fully forgiven yourself at a deep level. Your very low score on self-abasement doesn't mean great self-acceptance, but excessive self-rejection. Your moral sense is blunted. Let's work toward a proper self-acceptance, instead of burying all of the past and trying to walk away from it. No one can escape an outraged conscience."

She then told the entire story of her life. It involved a feeling of rejection in childhood and the search for a warm and loving relationship with many men. None of her relationships ever satisfied the deep need she felt.

Two years later, after participating in the group, she took the test again. This time she scored a healthier 40, evidence of a more sensitive conscience. Meanwhile she had grown spiritually and emotionally. There was objective evidence, too, of a new sense of self-worth. She was in the process of growing a new identity. She knew who she was. Instead of trying to bury her guilt feelings she had gotten them up, confessed them, talked them out privately, and felt fully forgiven by herself and by God.

How a Sense of Inferiority and False Guilt Is Created

One enormous barrier which prevents us from accepting and loving ourselves properly is self-rejection, which is simply another term for self-hate. This may result from feelings of inferiority set in motion in early childhood. A man in his early forties read his weekly slip one evening in the small group. It dealt with self-rejection. He said, "Yes, this is true. I have felt inadequate, or inferior, or guilty as long as I can remember. My parents told me a thousand times that I would never amount to anything. They said I was lazy, and that no one would ever employ me. I believed them! It was hammered into me day after day, year after year. What alternative does a child have but to believe his parents? If they had told me the world was flat, I would have believed them. Why not? They are the ultimate authorities."

He went on to describe the years of being beaten down and made to feel worthless. "It took me a long time to discover that my parents were wrong. I have succeeded fairly well in life, but way down deep I can still hear their voices. So I get this slip on self-rejection. I reject myself, I guess, because they made me feel worthless and unloved."

Like everyone else, he was the product of his environment. He had lived with this self-image for over forty years. We always tend to act in harmony with our self-image. He had fought his way out of total self-rejection, but he had not been able to eradicate completely the concept of himself as vaguely worthless, guilty, and inferior.

The group experience helped, in that the other eight or ten members mirrored his true worth. At first he could not accept at a feeling level their unconditional acceptance of him as an admirable person. Eventually it began to sink in, and he achieved a new self-confidence based on an entirely new self-image.

Satchel Paige once uttered a profound truth: "Don't look back. Something may be gaining on you!" There is wisdom in this, for to keep looking back in remorse is self-defeating. But it is only a partial truth. There is value in looking back to discover how we became the kind of persons we are. We do this, not to blame anyone, but to *rid ourselves of undeserved blame*.

I can see how my parents damaged me. There is no blame attached, for they, too, were damaged by their parents. I have passed it on, as it has been passed down through the ages from Adam to us.

We must go back and relive some of our childhood, as much as can be recalled. "Become as a little child" again, and reexperience every negative and positive memory. Try to dredge up the most painful memories, and talk them out with someone who understands, or in a sharing group. Let there be no blame. Your parents did their best, and you are doing your best, all things considered. The reliving of the past is an effort to dredge up all the pain-filled areas of your life, and dump them once and for all.

Beneath Our Hate Lies Our Capacity to Love

A woman in a Yokefellow group which I led said in one session, "I had to go back and hate my mother until all of the hate was burned up. The hatred was there, and there was no use denying it. I had to feel it, relive it. When I had hated her enough, then I could love her and forgive her."

The hostility which she felt toward her mother was hatred she felt as a child which could not then be expressed. To bury this is to deny it, and that is a lie to the self. When she could freely accept the fact that she had hated her mother, and still did, then she was free to love her. Her spiritual and emotional growth began when she could admit all of the negative feelings she had bottled up through the years. She could not achieve a new self-image until she had felt, and confessed, what she had denied for so many years. "One does not hate one's parents," she said. "A Christian loves everybody. Only I did hate my mother, and I didn't love everybody." Honesty with God, with oneself, and with others, is the all-essential first step toward spiritual growth.

I experienced a painful memory recently. It had lain buried for many years. I was in my third year of high school, and worked Saturdays in a grocery store. A black man made a purchase. He looked like he might have been a Pullman porter. I recalled hearing someone say that all Pullman porters were named George. As I handed him the package, I said, "Here you are, George." He looked at me for a moment, then said with quiet dignity, "My name isn't George."

As that long-forgotten memory rose to the surface, I experienced a surge of shame. I felt an irrational urge to try to find the man and apologize. He is dead by now, but the memory of my youthful blunder isn't. Because I felt wrong and ashamed at the time I simply pushed the memory down into the unconscious mind. Out of sight out of mind. Only it doesn't work that way. Time does not diminish guilt.

Am I guilty before God? No, not now, for my immediate sense of remorse was a silent confession and request for forgiveness. God forgives instantly. But I had not forgiven myself. I need not, in fact cannot, atone for that ancient wrong. But I can, for my own sake, make certain that I do not repeat it. I cannot put my arm around that particular man and say, "I'm sorry. That was stupid of me. Forgive me." But I can express positive regard for the next black person I meet. In fact, I cannot love myself properly until I do. Proper self-love, self-respect, a sense of identity, and self-worth all go together. I can recall a hundred things for which I feel a deeper sense of guilt, but that particular event, having been buried, brought a feeling of shame which told me that I had never forgiven myself.

Did Jesus Command Perfection?

Jesus' command, "You, therefore, must be perfect, as your heavenly Father is perfect,"[2] has troubled many persons. There is either a tendency to sweep it under the rug, since it is an impossibility, or to feel a generalized sense of guilt over the fact of one's failure. Yet it needs to be dealt with. What did Jesus mean?

As I see it, Jesus was setting a goal, not a requirement. God cannot be satisfied with imperfection. He is easy to please, hard to satisfy. The command is a goal, like his other difficult-to-attain standards. How can one love God with *all* of his heart, mind, soul, and strength? Who can attain the goal of loving one's enemies unconditionally? Who has attained the goal of consistently treating every other person precisely as he would like to be treated? Who among us can instantly and fully forgive every slight or injury?

No, Jesus did not set these as requirements or "laws" which, if violated, render us unworthy of God's love. They are goals, standards, toward which we are to strive. He was not trying to generate a deeper sense of guilt. He was saying, in effect, "This is what you would be like if you were truly human, if you were to let God be manifested in your life to the ultimate."

But from many sources, some valid and some invalid, we end up with a generalized sense of "being wrong," of moral failure. The paradox is that we are to reach for the ultimate, but accept the loving forgiveness of God when we fail, as we all do.

Formula for Self-Forgiveness

As a minister and counselor, I have dealt with many hundreds of people who seemed unable to accept and forgive themselves. Intellectual knowledge that God has forgiven one does not automatically provide self-acceptance and self-forgiveness. Eventually I evolved a formula to promote self-forgiveness. A portion of it I borrowed from Glenn Clark, and adapted it to the problem of achieving self-acceptance. It works like this:

To avoid falling into the trap of "either-or," of considering ourselves either "good" or "bad," "right" or wrong," one writes out a list similar to this:

I am neither good nor bad, I am both; and because God loves me, I will love myself properly.

I am neither guilty nor innocent, I am both; and because God forgives me, I will forgive myself.

I am neither loving nor hateful, I am both; and because God loves me, I will love myself properly.

I am neither pure nor impure, I am both; and because God accepts me, I will accept myself.

One can make up his own list of opposites. The underlying principle involved is this:

First, instead of labeling ourselves as either good or bad, we accept the paradox that we are neither, yet both. Jesus at no time termed anyone bad, and when someone called him "good," he rebuked him, saying, "No one is good but God."[3]

Second, by affirming and reaffirming this real truth about ourselves, and about God's love, we drop down into the emotional and spiritual nature a truth to counteract a lie. The lie is that we are "bad." The emotional structure accepts unquestioningly anything that it is told. It has no power of discernment, but in childlike simplicity accepts whatever is fed into it.

However, from infancy on up we have been led to believe that we were either "good" or "bad." "Have I been good today, Mommy?" We asked, because we knew we fell into one category or another. Mother and father did not always have the patience or insight to say, "Well, you have done some things today that weren't very nice, but that doesn't make *you* bad. I love you even when you have been disobedient."

Since we were so often led to believe that we were "bad," the inner self came to feel bad or wrong or inferior or worthless in some degree. To add to the damage done by those, who made us feel guilty, we accused ourselves—sometimes justly, often unjustly—of being stupid, or guilty. Therefore, it will take time to convince the emotional and spiritual self that we are not the guilty, sinful, worthless persons we have been led to believe.

The goal is to admit our errors and confess them, to rectify every possible wrong. Then we are to strive to forgive and accept ourselves.

I advise people suffering from a morbid sense of unworthiness, or guilt, to repeat their formula five times a day for three months. Some have it typed out and carry it about with them. Within ninety days, virtually anyone can have a new sense of being forgiven, and a new self-worth.

Not everyone needs this. It is chiefly intended for those who grew up in a judgmental or rejecting environment. A few fortunate persons are able to accept the forgiveness of God, forgive themselves, and move on. These are the ones who are likely to say, "God forgives you, now just forgive yourself. It's very simple!" But it is never that easy for people with a low sense of self-worth, or a morbid sense of guilt, or unworthiness. And their number is legion.

There is another group of people to whom this is all nonsense. They are the intellectualizers who are completely out of touch with their emotions. They usually do not know what they actually feel, having shut out that 85 percent of the self which is pure feeling. Yet they are often among the first to assert that they are in touch with all of their emotions, that they know themselves perfectly. They have an important reason for denying their true feelings. To admit them into consciousness is too threatening. It is much safer to live entirely on an intellectual plane.

131

Jerry was about thirty-five, highly intelligent, but not satisfied with his performance on the job, or in his marriage relationship. In a counseling session we went back over his early childhood. His parents were divorced when Jerry was seven. His father visited him regularly at first; but after he remarried, the visits were farther and farther apart. Eventually his father ceased to see Jerry, though he did send a Christmas card or a small gift each year.

His mother took a job, and Jerry understood quite well why it was necessary for his mother to work; but the fact remained that he came home from school day after day to an empty home. He buried his feelings of loneliness, and outwardly seemed gay and outgoing.

As he reviewed his childhood I detected a note of sadness in his voice, as though something had gone amiss back there, as indeed it had. Finally, when he was able to get in touch with his long-buried feelings, he became aware of the intense loneliness he felt as a child, and the deep sense of abandonment he felt when his father ceased visiting him. Rejection registers the same as guilt: "If I am rejected, it must be because I am no good," is the feeling. Now at thirty-five Jerry was facing the fact that both his job and his marriage were threatened because of something in his personality which he could not put his finger on. Eventually he came to see what it was.

He was simply projecting onto his fellow employees, and onto his wife and children, the unresolved anger he had felt as a child over being abandoned. He was not even aware of the anger until I helped him relive the period of his life when it happened.

It is never enough simply to discuss calmly such experiences. They must be felt out, relived and reexperienced at a deep feeling level. Jerry had to do just that; and often as we went back over his childhood, he would stop to gain control of himself. When he learned that he need no longer control these emotions, but could weep them out, the healing began. He wept the unshed tears of the past, and with them came a great relief. He had denied to himself that he was lonely or rejected. At last he gave up the pretense and let his true feelings come to the surface. It was very painful, of course, but it was a healing experience.

The release enabled him to be honest with his wife, and admit that he was not the strong, controlled, all-sufficient person he had pretended to be. He began to function differently at work. The buried anger of childhood had crippled the adult and made him cold and distant. Now he became a much warmer person who related more easily to others.

Because of a lifelong feeling of inferiority, which he kept well hidden, Jerry did not feel that God loved him, or could forgive him. His father had let him down, and now as an adult Jerry was not always sure that he believed in God. He had difficulty repeating the Lord's Prayer. The word "Father" stuck in his throat. I suggested that he never use the term "Father" as applied to God. Then I gave him the formula for self-acceptance and self-forgiveness. I assured him that if he would faithfully repeat the affirmation five times a day for ninety days he would feel differently about himself. He reported later that, though he had missed some days, he had worked at it diligently most of the time. "And it worked," he added. "One day I started to repeat my formula and suddenly I thought, 'I don't need this any more. I believe it down deep.' And everything is better both at home and at work."

The word "prayer" has an automatic connotation of "supplication," of asking for something, of beseeching God; but the most powerful prayer is one of affirmation. Read the twenty-third Psalm and look for any supplication. There isn't any. It is simply a prayer of affirmation, in which the psalmist affirms to his own soul what he knows intellectually about God.

A law of physics holds that two objects cannot occupy the same space at the same time. A psychological corollary is that two ideas cannot occupy one's attention at the same time. If one's emotional structure is filled with feelings of guilt, or unworthiness, or inferiority, or hate, then it is impossible to entertain feelings of being forgiven, or being worthy in God's sight, or to experience the emotion of love. It is going to be one or the other, or at best an unsatisfying mixture.

A variation of the formula used by Jerry applies to the matter of love and hate. When we dislike or hate someone, it is difficult even to *want* to love them.

"I've tried to love my mother," said one of our group members, "but I can't seem to bring it off. I no sooner get a faint feeling of warmth for her, then she does something that sets me off again, and I don't even want to be around her. All I can feel is hostility, and it makes me feel guilty not to have at least some positive feelings about my own mother."

I gave her the formula: "I *want* to want to accept and love my mother." This going back one step made it possible for her to begin. It took her some months; but as she dropped that prayer of affirmation down into her deep inner self, she observed that her mother seemed less objectionable, less demanding. She kept at her daily formula until she arrived at the point where she no longer felt antipathy, simply compassion and love for another human being.

"I now see my mother," she said, "not as my Mom who interferes in everything, but as another person, and I love the good in her. I treat her as just another individual, person to person, and we have established a good relationship. She is no longer able to make me feel like her little girl, which always made me mad, and I don't feel that she is my 'Mommy' whom I am duty-bound to love and adore. I see her as a mixed-up person who was damaged in childhood by her environment, just as I was. We get along fine. She's changed!"

What Is The Deepest Human Urge?

Jesus did not ask people if they wanted him to make them holy, but he did on occasion ask, "Would you like to be made *whole?*" To be made whole is to become integrated, unified, to end the inner conflict.

Freud felt that the sex drive was man's deepest urge. Adler, one of his disciples, broke with him over this concept, insisting that man's deepest urge is to achieve power, to compensate for childhood feelings of inferiority. It was he who coined the term "inferiority complex." Viktor Frankl later asserted that neither of these is man's basic urge, but that "the will to meaning" is the fundamental drive.

There is validity to all of these propositions, but, at the risk of seeming presumptuous, I disagree somewhat with these eminent gentlemen. The basic, fundamental drive underlying all of the others is *the urge to discover one's true identity, and to be fulfilled.* Fulfilling the love-sex drive is important. It is important to compensate for our feelings of inferiority and inadequacy. It is terribly important to discover meaning in life. But underlying all these urges at a much deeper level is the God-implanted urge to find out who we are, to discover our true identity. Then this newly discovered identity, or "self," must be fulfilled.

Hedonism assumes that one can be fulfilled through physical gratification. Mysticism holds that one can be fulfilled only through a spiritual union with God. Adler's assumption is that one reaches his basic goal through achievement, and a consequent sense of being worthwhile, no longer inferior. Millions have broken their hearts and ruined their lives trying out these dead-end streets. The will to meaning, postulated by Frankl, comes nearer, but it is not the ultimate.

Few if any ever achieve *complete* satisfaction in life. A state of constant happiness is a myth. One must settle for that cousin of happiness, contentment; and no one is ever fully content until he has discovered his true identity, until he can say: "I am a god; I am the king of my own inner kingdom. I am in charge. Because I am made in the image of God, I am an immortal spirit consisting of the same essence as the Father. I, the imperishable Self, cannot die any more than God can die. God seeks to fulfill himself through me."

"God is at work in you, both to will and to work for his good pleasure."[4] What he seeks to accomplish in us is "good"—the ultimate good, the only real and lasting good we shall ever know. He seeks our fulfillment. He wants to express himself through us. As we let down the barriers of pride—the father of all sins—God is enabled to fulfill his glorious purpose in and through us.

The paradox is that though "we are in charge"—that is, responsible—God makes his infinite resources available. He does not seek to control us, simply to guide us. In fact, the one thing he will not do is to control us, but he does seek to guide and empower us to make his limitless resources available to us.

I went to sleep one night asking the question, "What is the meaning of life?" I awoke the next morning with something running through my mind repetitiously. It was "Jesus, joy of man's desiring." I found the recording of Bach's lovely chorale and listened while I pondered the meaning. Was this the ultimate meaning of life—to turn one's life over to Christ, and then receive it back again, cleansed, forgiven? Was it to desire the spirit of Christ so earnestly that life somehow took on new meaning? Is ultimate joy to be found in perfect obedience to Christ? If so, how does one achieve all this?

One morning months later I awoke with the phrase running through my mind, "In everything God works for good with those who love him."⁵ In *everything!* That would include physical, mental, spiritual—the whole gamut. All of life is included in that—work, play, love, worship. And if he is truly at work, gently, relentlessly seeking to fulfill himself through us, what in the world prevents us from letting him accomplish that? Fulfillment, becoming a *real* person, a whole person, consists then in letting God take over. Take over? Forget it! That means loss of identity, the giving up of our autonomy.

God Seeks to Guide, Not Control

Here is a paradox: how to accept total responsibility for our own actions, to be literally the "king of our own inner kingdom," yet be totally subservient to God. Yet the paradox is not as threatening or complex as it seems. A simple parallel comes to mind. In a manufacturing plant nearby, some ten thousand persons are employed. The president of the corporation is in charge, and responsible for the overall operation. Employees are given responsibilities, general instructions, and expected to perform according to some established principles. No one supervises their every move. Many are given wide latitude in making decisions, depending upon the type of work assigned them.

Each worker has autonomy within a general framework. They are not controlled or forced. Failure to attain a recognized standard in the performance of their duties could result in their dismissal; but they are free either to follow the company rules or to disobey them.

The president of the firm needs them as much as they need him. They are mutually interdependent. The president assumes ultimate responsibility, but the individual worker has his responsibility, too. Each worker at a lathe, or in the sales or shipping department, has autonomy and freedom within limits. Each is responsible, and in charge of his own particular task. But working with him and making avail-

136

able all that he needs to do the job well is the president of the firm.

I envision God as being unwilling to control us, or to take responsibility for our actions. He is available for fellowship (why not bring him into our laughter, our joys as well as our sorrows and crises?), for guidance, and as the ultimate Source of all things.

Growth is always gradual, and often it involves pain, or at least struggle. Growth toward the goal of becoming a God-centered person often involves the pain of giving up our pride. It involves learning how to give and receive love, and above all, to obey the teachings and spirit of Jesus. When we succeed, he rejoices. When we fail, and fail we will, he forgives and awaits our return. And as he waits, I know for a certainty that there is a smile on his face—a smile of rejoicing and welcome. We have come home at last. That's all that matters.

9.

Love Is What It's All About

> "We cannot endure hearing one criticized whom we love or admire. We cannot endure hearing one praised whom we despise."
> —C. GILLETTE

JEFFREY LANSDOWN died when he was five years old. He was beaten to death by his stepfather. As reported by the press, Jeffrey's nude, animal-ravaged remains were found at the bottom of an embankment near a desert road. For three weeks prior to his death, the boy had suffered savage mistreatment at the hands of Ronald Foquet, the stepfather. The mother claimed that she dared not interfere because she feared he would harm her other children. Jeffrey had been polishing one of his stepfather's shoes, and it had fallen out of the window to the street below. The mother could not retrieve it because her husband would not permit her to leave the house when he was away. Later in the day the boy accidentally upset a can of paint.

When Foquet discovered that one of his shoes was missing, he beat the boy mercilessly with a belt and ordered him to stand in a corner. Later, when he found the spilled can of paint, he beat him again, and refused to allow him to eat dinner. In succeeding days the boy was beaten, pounded with fists, and forced to crawl around on the floor until his knees bled. The stepfather tied Jeffrey to a doorknob so that he could not sit or lie down. Finally he stepped on him. Later police asked the mother what her son had said when Foquet had threatened to kill him. The mother sobbed, "Jeff just said, 'Daddy, I love you.' "

How is it possible to account for such sadistic savagery? What had so warped the man's mind that he could beat a helpless, innocent child to death and then dispose of his battered body as if it were garbage?

Still another question haunts one's mind. At the other end of the spectrum of human emotions, what was it in little Jeffrey's nature that enabled him to say to the man who had beaten him for nearly three weeks and then threatened to kill him, "Daddy, I love you?"

Every human being born into this world is created with the innate capacity to give and receive love. God, whose other name is Love, has planted in our hearts the need to love and be loved. This is part of our divinity, that portion of each individual which is created "in the image of God," in his spiritual likeness.

Love is what it's all about. Thinking of the whole spectrum of love as caring, concern, positive regard, compassion, friendship, affection, romantic love, agape-love, benevolence—this is the attribute which is most certainly one of the strongest human drives.

"Love is the medicine for the healing of the world," said Dr. Karl Menninger, which is simply an echo of Jesus' statement that the supreme good is to love God with one's whole nature, to love one's neighbor, and to love oneself properly.

Learning to Accept Love Can Be Difficult

I met a very lonely young man of twenty-four at a retreat. He made an appointment to see me, and told me something of his early life. Both at home and at school he had experienced a sense of utter rejection. Because he was timid and unable to defend himself, he was the victim of many taunts and jokes. He had always felt alone and friendless. At the office where he worked a sadistic fellow-worker made life miserable for him. No one stood up for him.

I encouraged him to join a Yokefellow group, where ten or twelve persons, meeting weekly, could share their feelings and seek emotional and spiritual growth. In time he was able to share some of his lifelong pain, and the group members responded with concern and affection. However, he could not believe that they really cared. Never having experienced love, he could not recognize or believe in it when it was offered.

At one session I asked him to stand at the end of the room. I then blindfolded him, and told him that each member of the group was going to approach him and express whatever they felt toward him in some physical way. I said, "They may express a negative feeling by giving you a push; or they may express a positive feeling by shaking hands with you, embracing you, or in any other way they care to." He said, "Dr. Osborne, this is very frightening!"

The first person to rise and approach him was a woman. She put her arms around him tenderly, hugged him, and kissed him on the cheek. A man put both hands on the young man's shoulders, then gave him a big bear hug. A young woman, who had known rejection herself, went over and kissed him gently. Another woman hugged him. A man shook his hand and with genuine warmth. All of the others in the group expressed positive feeling for him in similar ways.

When I removed the blindfold, the young man stood there immobilized. He wanted to cry, but restrained himself. "It is unbelievable. I simply can't believe it," he finally said, and sat down stunned.

At the conclusion of the group session, as though to reinforce their silent expression of concern and love, fully half the group took the trouble to go to him again and express their feelings verbally.

At the beginning of this decade some students and counselors at the University of California at Berkeley expressed the opinion that 80 percent or more of the students felt alienated and lonely. It is probable that most adults experience to some degree the same sense of alienation from God, from others, and from themselves.

This alienation, resulting in loneliness and feeling of rejection, is the very opposite of agape-love. There is a built-in, threefold need which every human experiences: the need for acceptance, approval, and affection. A person may survive on one or two of these, but he will always experience a haunting sense of loneliness, of being unfulfilled, if he does not receive all three.

141

"Give and It Will Be Given to You"

In a sense we are all "tin cuppers"—going around with a tin cup with holes in the bottom, silently begging to be loved, to be accepted, to be approved of. Jesus indicated that this approach is all wrong. He said, "Give, and it will be given to you."[1] It's up to you, he was saying. You're in charge. *Give* love and you will receive it!

I saw this dramatically illustrated in a Yokefellow group of twelve persons. One of the group members, a young woman in her twenties, had never been loved as a child. She had experienced periods of intense depression and hopelessness, and felt totally unloved. Nothing that anyone said could convince her that she was acceptable. The rejection in childhood had been so severe that she could not believe in love, even when it was offered.

In one group session when she had spoken of her utter loneliness, I asked her to go to each person in the group and express verbally some positive feeling. She got up reluctantly, and rather stiffly began to go around the circle, speaking hesitantly to the first two or three. Then it became a little easier, and she began to touch the person to whom she spoke.

Halfway around the circle she became more confident. "Genevieve, I think you're a great person. I like you," she said, and kissed her.

"Frank," she said, as she touched him on the shoulder, "I—I've rejected you because you remind me of my father, whom I hated, but down deep I appreciate you a lot."

Kissing the next person, she said, "Addie, you're a wonderful person."

"John, I like you." She reached down and gave him a gentle hug. She was beginning to feel more deeply.

"Fred, I'm fond of you but I never know how to express it." She squeezed his hand and moved on to the next person.

"Jeannie, I love you," and she kissed her.

With each succeeding expression she became less self-conscious, more open and real. Finally, when she completed the circle, she sat down and burst into tears. Between sobs, she said over and over, "I love you all!" Later she said, "For the first time I could believe the group loved me, after I expressed my love for each of you."

My wife and I were guests at a buffet dinner given for a newly arrived government official from the Middle East. The seventy-five or more guests were gathered in the huge living room with a magnificent view of San Francisco Bay. I found myself listening to a chatty little woman whom I could scarcely hear above the babble voices. Everyone was talking animatedly, but no one appeared to be saying anything of any particular significance, and I was frankly bored.

A distinguished-looking man caught my gaze. He was standing alone in the middle of the crowded room, staring abstractedly out across the bay. His face looked so familiar that I thought for a moment it was someone I had known. Then I recognized him. He was a famous World War II admiral, whose name had been a household word during the war. He looked genuinely lonely. Tiring of the inane trivia being poured into my ear, I excused myself, intending to go over and visit with the admiral. But with newly arriving guests the crowd became so densely packed that I could not make my way to the center of the room where stood a lonely, world-famous military figure, surrounded by people too preoccupied with their own banalities to notice him. Even the internationally famous are not immune, I thought.

Love is not just an emotion; it is also an action. Jesus did not command us to *feel* any particular way, but to *act* in certain ways. He did not urge us to feel affection for our enemies, but to love them—meaning to act toward them with unconditional concern and positive regard.

Two minister friends and I fell to discussing events early in life which had influenced us. One of them said, "In the vast three thousand-member church where I grew up, I felt that they were interested in my soul, but not in me as a person. I resolved that if I ever became a minister I would try to show concern for the whole person, not just for his soul." He has made good on that early promise. Everyone who knows him feels his genuine concern for them as persons. He is a truly loving person.

I related an incident which left its mark on me. I was a scared, sixteen-year-old college freshman in need of a part-time job in order to support myself. Having grown up in the church, it seemed natural to me to turn for help to the senior minister of a large church near the campus. I can still see his cool, impersonal gaze. I told him I needed to find a part-time job, and wondered if he could suggest any leads. He looked vague, and admitted that he didn't know just what one would do. "But," he said, "if I can be of service to you in some other way, just let me know." I was in and out of his office in less than sixty seconds; and as I turned to go, he went back to his reading. My feeling was that even if he could provide no practical help, he could have expressed some interest or concern. I felt nothing but indifference on his part; and as I walked away from the church, I resolved that when I became a minister, I would listen with interest to anyone who had a problem and do what I could to help. I may not always have made good on that, but in a sense I am grateful for the rejection I received that day. It made me more sensitive to human need.

The third in our trio of ministers related an experience of his. When he decided to enter the ministry, he went to his pastor and discussed it with him. The older man took plenty of time to visit with him, and gave him much valuable counsel. "It meant a lot to me to know that he genuinely cared about me, and I have never forgotten it. I've tried to pass that on."

To Be Loved, Be What You Want Others to Be

In one of our Yokefellow groups the discussion turned to love. Several spoke of having felt unloved as children. Someone referred to the fact that we learn to give and receive love through having been loved in childhood. Another asked, "Why can't people be more loving?"

A woman who had not shared in the discussion said, "I asked myself that question one day. It was in those very words: why can't people be more loving? Then I went into a period of meditation, and suddenly a gentle inner voice said, 'Be what you want others to be.' I tried that and it worked. The first thing I discovered was that I became far less critical and judgmental."

A wife whose husband was highly critical of her house-keeping said that her husband once wrote, "I love you," with his finger on a dusty table top. She said, "Of course I didn't feel loved; I felt criticized. I think if I felt more loved I could become motivated to be a better housekeeper."

Criticism, no matter how expressed or how well deserved, is always perceived as an attack. The more sensitive one is the more devastating the attack is felt to be. How, then, can two people, or a family or a group, operate if they are not permitted to express honest feelings?

There is a higher principle than the law of honesty. To be honest may be admirable, but to be loving is supreme. One may say, "I have to be honest. I always say just what I think without beating around the bush." Then comes the devastating criticism which the recipient usually perceives as an attack. To speak and act in love is more important than to express all of one's honest opinions. We need not go to the opposite extreme and evade the issue, equivocate, and placate. There is obviously a time for directness and a forthright expression of how we feel about a given subject. But the Apostle Paul has given us a guideline here: "Love is patient and kind. . . ."[2]

Harold was a deeply frustrated man when I first met him. He had just lost his job with a large insurance firm, where he had been a vice president. He had been let out with the simple statement that he just didn't "fit in." Twice before he had worked his way almost to the top in other firms, only to have the rug pulled out from under him. He spent two or three years in one of our Yokefellow groups while he worked at a fairly menial position to support himself and his family. The group took one of the spiritual growth inventories which are often used by groups originating in the West Coast Yokefellow Center. A total of eleven slips were received, one every two weeks. One of the first ones Harold received read as follows:

You have some aggressive feelings which are not being fully expressed, or if they are, they are making you unhappy. Many people repress their aggression, and then suffer from either depression, or some physical symptom. In your case, your test results show that you are excessively depressed at times. It is important that you get your hostile feelings out in the open. Discuss them in the group. Be frank and honest in admitting that you feel hostility at times. In discussing it, let your full feelings be felt. You can handle hostility better after you have faced it, and after you discover that people will accept you even when you show resentment or hostility. Ask yourself, "What have I to lose by verbalizing my hostility in the group? What is the main reason for my fear of doing this? How did I acquire the habit of burying my aggression?"

The slip also contained some specific suggestions as to what to read in a book the group was using. It concluded with the statement, "We learn to cope with our discoveries about ourselves in the daily Quiet Time: 'Thou wilt keep him in perfect peace, whose mind is stayed on thee.' "[3]

Harold denied having any unusual amount of hostility. Most of the group agreed with him. He was so spontaneously witty that it was a pleasure to be around him— except for one thing: though his wit bubbled up constantly from some inner pool of humor, after most of his flashes people would laugh hysterically, only to discover later that someone was bleeding from a rapier thrust.

Too, he gave dogmatic, unsolicited advice and opinions on virtually every conceivable subject. He offered simplistic answers to complex problems, and seemed to feel that he was an authority on any given topic, even in fields where he had no knowledge or experience.

I began to understand why Harold had been "getting the shaft." Initially, in a group his wit was fairly gentle. The better he got to know people, the sharper he became. I could see how, as he became more and more secure in his job, the more deadly his humor would become, until it was unendurable.

Little by little Harold began to discover that his humor was a defense mechanism—delightful most of the time, but devastating and self-defeating in the long run. His wit concealed hostility he had buried in his unconscious mind. He was totally unaware that he was a hostile person.

After a year or so in the group, he discovered the power of love, and no longer kept people at arm's length with his wit. He learned to use it with more discretion, and without a barb.

One group member said, "When I was the object of your humor, Harold, I usually laughed my head off, but by the time I stopped laughing I'd find my throat had been cut. It felt so good to laugh that I didn't mind—for the moment. But later, I got to resenting you and fearing those funny, devastating barbs. I can see why people would enjoy your company, because I do; but maybe in the top echelons they don't enjoy having their throats cut even when it's hilariously funny."

Harold just smiled. He had begun to learn to love, and to permit himself to be loved, and no longer felt the same need to attack under the guise of humor.

Listening Is an Act of Love

A woman who came in twice weekly for counseling proved to be a compulsive talker. She had had nine years with a psychiatrist, and possessed great insight, but her problems remained unresolved. In her initial session she began to talk animatedly, and then with considerable irritation asked, "Could you turn off that music? It bothers me."

I said, "Of course. Not everyone likes background music, no matter how soft." I turned off the music and looked at her.

She said, "I know why I wanted it off. I want your complete attention. No one ever listened to me when I was a child. No one *ever* listened! That's why I talk so much now. I'm making up for lost time."

Listening can be an act of love. Who listens to children? Parents instruct them, lecture them, order them around, scold them, but seldom does one find a parent who will take time just to sit down and *listen*. Or if the parent listens, and detects something in the child's thinking that needs to be straightened out, that's the signal to start lecturing.

The father of two teenagers said, "I've discovered that any statement I make to my kids over three sentences in length is a lecture, and they tune me out. After those first two or three sentences I might just as well shut up. I didn't like lectures when I was a kid, and I can understand why they don't like them."

Listening to a friend, to one's mate, or to any other person, can be a genuine act of love. It is perfectly normal to want to interrupt with some gem of wisdom, or an observation; but if you want to express love, *listen!* Listen with the third ear; listen to the plea behind the words: "Hear me, show an interest in me, let me know that you care enough about me to look at me and give me your undivided attention. Don't argue with me in an effort to show me where I'm wrong. I feel wrong and unworthy most of the time, and if you reject what I am saying, you make me feel more unworthy. Just listen!"

Taken literally and to the extreme, this would suggest becoming a passive, silent, patient martyr putting up with earth's compulsive talkers without protest, or even sharing in the conversation. Obviously, this is not implied. But to listen with interest, instead of waiting with ill-concealed impatence for a semi-colon, is a manifestation of interest and concern, and this is a facet of love.

There is the classic story of a movie star at a Hollywood party who talked animatedly for a solid hour about herself. Finally she turned to her partner and said, "But enough about me. Let's talk about you. What did *you* think of my last picture?" One need not become a victim of egocentric compulsive talkers in order to manifest love and concern. A proper self-love entitles one to avoid those deadly bores.

Listening in the Family

A common complaint of wives is: "My husband won't talk. He's uncommunicative. I'm dying for someone to talk to." Husbands who do not communicate fall into two categories; those who are innately incapable of carrying on an intelligent conversation, and those who have been turned off by criticism, argument, or an overtalkative wife.

One husband reported that his wife complained of his being withdrawn and uncommunicative. He said, "I do talk very little at home. I am much more spontaneous and talkative at work. I don't get shot down and criticized there. I must appear morose and uninterested at home, but I can't help it. At the office we have more fun and hilarity in a week than we do at home in six months. We don't tear each other apart at work. We accept each other. I don't feel accepted at home."

Tragically, the less he communicated at home, the more she complained, thus compounding the situation.

The other side of the coin is the husband, one of the army of the quiet un-dead, who sits in front of the television set night after night and over the weekend, refusing to meet his wife's need for adult conversation. Even the most withdrawn husband could, without too much strain, ask his wife about her day, listen with interest, and validate her feelings. This in itself is an act of love.

In too many instances to be ignored I have observed that both men and women often marry someone with the same type of personality as the parent of the opposite sex. A man marries a dominating, cold unresponsive woman. At a totally unconscious level he has sought out a woman much like his mother, and then tries to make her into a *loving* mother such as he never knew but needed. A woman often marries a mild, passive man much like her father. She may mistake his quietness for quiet strength, only to discover later that is uncommunicative and weak like her father. Unconsciously she is trying to re-create and relive the past and make her husband over into the kind of father she desired.

Changes can be made in such marriages—but not in the other person; only in us. If we will change, we will usually find that others change in reaction to us.

A young married woman told me in a counseling session that she would be happy if her husband would fall in love with someone else and leave her. "I'm fed up to here," she said. "He's inattentive, uncommunicative, and generally impossible." I knew her husband, and could readily sympathize with her.

Three months later she reported. "We've never been happier. He's changed so completely you'd never know him. He brought me flowers this week. He plays with the children, and helps around the house. He shows an interest in me, and in what I'm feeling."

I was frankly amazed. True, we had been working on a specific program which involved some changes in her. She was to make no demands, offer no criticism, be gentle, loving and understanding, regardless of his attitude. She read a book which outlined some of the things she was to work on. Within a month there was a radical change in her husband. In three months the transformation was unbelievable. They were in love again. Love-in-action had triumphed.

When Parents Seem Incapable of Love

It is not always easy for parents to love their children unconditionally and consistently; and it is equally hard for many people to feel genuine love for their parents. Some individuals feel guilty because they are unable to love their parents as much as they feel they should.

A young woman said in a group session, "I received no love from my parents, at least not in the form that I could accept. They are both very limited persons, and ever since I left home I have been going back at every opportunity, unconsciously trying to win from them the love I never received as a child.

"Just recently I went back for a visit. It was dreadful. My mother treated me as if I were five years old instead of thirty. I found myself trying to win her love, but she has none to give. My father is a dead loss. I came away in tears. It will be a long time before I go back again."

She is understandably frustrated, but she will have to find love elsewhere rather than from parents who are incapable of giving it. With her whole being she needs to be validated, cared for, cherished. The inner child of the past still cries out for love.

A minister shared with his congregation the account of a psychiatrist's family therapy session involving a mother who was uptight and a religious fanatic. The father was a weak, wisecracking type of individual. There were twins, age fourteen, a boy seventeen, and a girl, nineteen. In the therapsy session the psychiatrist centered around the tension existing between the seventeen-year-old son and his mother. The boy admitted that he could hardly stand the sight of his mother. She was bitter, and felt that her love had been rejected.

Finally the psychiatrist spoke. Turning to the young man he said, "Why don't you just pack up and leave?"

"I'm too young to do that. Besides, she is my mother."

"Well," said the therapist, "if you can't leave home, why don't you just put a lock on your door, and go to your room and get away from your mother?"

"She's my mother, and I don't think I could do a thing like that in my own home."

The other members of the family began to feel some hostility toward the psychiatrist. "What kind of a therapist are you, anyway?" the father asked, "giving advice like that? What kind of relationship do you have with *your* mother?"

"I haven't talked to my mother in twenty years," the pyschiatrist replied.

"And you're trying to help us with *our* family relationships, and you haven't spoken to your mother in twenty years?"

"Well," the psychiatrist said, "it's like this. The person who bore me, the one you call my mother, is quite well, and getting along fine. She is a good friend now; not a mother. We get along beautifully. I don't have a father or mother anymore; just good friends."

Love Your Enemies

Many people, I find, experience mild to severe guilt because of hostility they feel toward their parents, or because they are unable to love them devotedly. The command, "Honor your father and your mother,"[4] has confused many. The command says nothing about love, and particularly nothing about affection which we cannot turn on and off like a faucet. Besides, the commandment to honor one's parents applies primarily to children and young people, not to mature adults. An adult whose parents are not easy to get along with can always express positive regard.

When Jesus called upon us to love our enemies,[5] he was not suggesting approval or affection, but unconditional positive regard and concern, regardless of personal feelings about them. The enemy we are to love in this manner may well be a relative—parent, husband, wife, brother, or sister. The enemy may be one's self, or that part of the self that is unacceptable. We are not commanded to love the evil within ourselves or another, but to love the total person, as God does, to love the damaged, warped, sinful self at the core of which resides the spirit of God.

A deputy sheriff in our country told how he and three others took a violently insane man to a mental institution. He fought them every inch of the way. It required the full strength of all four men to control him. They dragged the struggling man down the hall and pushed him into a chair. Three deputies held him there. A cleaning woman hearing the noise came to observe.

As the insane man continued to struggle, the cleaning woman went over and touched him gently. He looked up at her and saw a woman with a look of deep compassion. She put her hand on his shoulder. He relaxed and ceased to struggle. Someone brought her a chair. She sat beside him and began to talk gently, soothingly.

The deputies relaxed their grip. For half an hour the cleaning woman talked to him as one would talk to a child. His whole body relaxed. He could feel her love and concern, and was responding to it. Finally, he was led away by a nurse. He went calmly. Love had done what the strength of four men could not accomplish.

Humanity vs. Individuals

It is much easier to love humanity than to love individual persons. This is true both in and out of families. A high school girl attended a peace rally where she held hands with various members of minority groups, and sang hymns as they resolutely faced the police lines. On the way home she stopped at the home of a neighbor. She was ecstatic. "Love, love—it's wonderful! We should envelop the entire world in love. People of all races and countries should join in the great brotherhood of man."

"That's beautiful," someone said. "Now, why don't you go home and tell your mother and father that you love them?"

She looked scornful and replied, "Oh, *them*. I can't *stand* them!"

A comic strip has a youngster proclaiming his love for his girl friend: "I love you with all my heart. I love you more than life itself, and would move mountains and change the course of mighty rivers for you."

She asks, "Would you come over Saturday and help me clean my junk out of the garage?"

"I hate people who take advantage," he replies.

A young married woman related her experience with a minister who had called at her home. "He found me in a depressed mood, and I was crying when I opened the door. He looked concerned, and I told him about some of my problems. I went on crying while I was talking to him, and he seemed to become more and more uncomfortable. Finally he said, 'If I can ever help you in any way let me

152

know,' and got up to leave. I said, 'I need help right now,' but he was already at the door. I haven't been back to church since. I know I am wrong to feel as I do, but if that's all the church has to offer, I don't need it."

Arthur Hoppe, who writes a column in the *San Francisco Chronicle*, told in one of his columns of his experience in "adopting" a Vietnam orphan. He had joined the Foster Parents' Plan and become a foster parent. He was assigned a child numbered 8944—one Nguyen Khac Trung. He had been sent a photograph of Trung, and as he looked at it he became alarmed. He asked himself why he had allowed himself to become burdened with another human being with whom he would have to correspond.

Six months passed. Then a letter from New York regretfully informed him that Trung's village had been overrun and contact with the boy had been lost. "I should have felt grief and worry; instead I felt relieved—a bit guilty, but mostly relieved. After all, I had never known the boy." He conveniently forgot all about him.

Two years later a letter came, written in elegant Vietnamese script, with a translation attached: "Dear Father, I thank you for last month's gift, which were 950 $VN (U.S. $8.11), two bars of soap and a towel. . . ."

His letter was bright and chatty. He had been ill, but was better. His sisters were fine. He asked for a picture of his foster father, "so that whenever I think of you, I'll take it out and look at it."

"My initial reaction was one of anger," wrote Arthur Hoppe. "I felt trapped. I knew that for years to come I would have to write regularly to the boy, send him presents and worry about his welfare—not so much out of generosity as out of guilt. You can't abandon a child.

"So I resented this new child, cluttering up my neat, comfortable, well-ordered life. But now it has grown late. The lights of our affluent society have come on outside my window. I have slowly come to see what a fitting penance this is.

"How easy it has been all these years to be intellectually concerned with the fate of the seventeen million people of South Vietnam. And how terribly hard it is to be honestly concerned with the fate of just one of them. God give me the grace to do it well."[6]

A child never experiences any greater fear than that of being abandoned, or unloved by his parents. He desperately fears being ignored or rejected. In fact, a child derives his only sense of identity from being loved, cared for, noticed, approved. Without such affirmation a child grows up with little sense of being worthwhile, thus with no sense of identity.

We never outgrow this need. The degrees we award and honors we bestow, the titles we give and receive, are all adult counterparts of the love the child needed. We seek it, hunger for it, and are often warped if denied it. We are "tin cuppers," waiting for someone to fill our cups. Love can come in the form of approval, of being noticed, listened to, complimented. At a deeper level we need affection as well as approval and acceptance. Denied love, we suffer at some deep level.

Even when we do find love and affirmation we may stifle and thwart it. Kahlil Gibran's counsel to two lovers is equally applicable to the relationship between any two persons: "Let there be spaces in your togetherness." He points out that "the oak tree and the cypress grow not in each other's shadow."⁷ Intimacy and mutual love need not imply a cloying, excessive togetherness or dependency. Whether in marriage, friendship, or any other relationship, each person must retain his individuality. Ideally, love does not coerce, but provides an atmosphere in which the other is free to grow toward wholeness.

Instead of seeking love so eagerly, clutching at it, as though it would elude our grasp, or withdrawing from life because love is denied us, Jesus told us to *give* love. "Give, and it will be given to you; good measure, pressed down, shaken together, running over, will be put into your lap."⁸ If you are not receiving your share of love, *start giving*. Give love, approval, acceptance; give time or energy or money or friendship; give whatever the need seems to suggest. *Give!*

There is no need for you to wait outside the window of life, looking in hungrily where love is being experienced in abundance. Open the door and walk in, not asking but offering friendship, affirmation, good will, forgiveness, as the situation may suggest.

It's all up to you. *You are in charge!*

Notes

Preface

1. Gal. 5:17, RSV.
2. John 10:34, RSV
3. Rev. 1:6.

Chapter 1: You're in Charge

1. John 3:17, RSV.
2. Num. 32:23, RSV.
3. John 15:11, NEB.
4. Ps. 119:18.
5. Ps. 119:165.
6. Phil. 2:13, RSV.
7. Gen. 1:28; 3:3, RSV.
8. Job. 13:15.

Chapter 2: Who Am I?

1. Gal. 5:17.
2. Rom. 7:19, 24, RSV.
3. Luke 17:21.
4. *New English Bible.*
5. John 14:1.
6. Luke 12:57, Phillips.
7. Robert Browning, *Paracelsus,* I, "Paracelsus Aspires."
8. John 9:5.
9. 1 John 1:6.
10. John 8:36, RSV.
11. Exod. 3:11.

12. Rom. 8:14.
13. Phil. 1:12, RSV.
14. John 7:17, Phillips.
15. 1 John 1:7, RSV.

Chapter 3: How You Can Receive Forgiveness

1. Ps. 51:5.
2. Luke 12:48, RSV.
3. Luke 15:11–24.
4. Matt. 25:30, 41, 46.
5. Heb. 9:27.
6. James 4:17, NEB.
7. Luke 6:27–28.
8. Matt. 22:35–40; Rom. 13:8–10; Gal. 5:14.
9. Mark 2:17, NEB.

Chapter 4: What a Great Time to Be Alive!

1. Quoted in *The San Francisco Chronicle.*
2. 1 Kings 19:14.
3. Rev. 21:3, 4, RSV.

Chapter 5: Love, Not Legalism

1. John 13:34, RSV.
2. John 8:36, RSV.
3. Philem. 2; see also Rom. 16:5, 23; Col. 4:15.
4. Gal. 5:22, 23, RSV.
5. Rom. 14:17, RSV.
6. John 15:11, RSV.
7. John 16:24, RSV.
8. Acts. 13:52, RSV.
9. John 14:10.
10. This and the following material is from *Life*, May 1, 1970.
11. John 13:34, RSV.

Chapter 6: Prayer Isn't What You Say

1. Matt. 9:29, RSV.
2. Acts. 14:9–10, NEB.
3. "Prayer is the soul's sincere desire," James Montgomery.
4. Isa. 30:15, RSV.

1z4387